School
Experience

CHRISTIANITY

John Mayled
Janet Green

GCSE Religious Studies

Hodder & Stoughton

A MEMBER OF THE HODDER HEADLINE GROUP

OCR

RECOGNISING ACHIEVEMENT

The publishers would like to thank the following individuals, institutions and companies for permission to reproduce copyright illustrations in this book:

Alamy Images: p4 l and r, and p5 r (Christine Osbourne), p5 l and p108 b (Robert Harding World Imagery), p30 b (Sami Sarkis), p48 (Reichhold), p85 (Brian Lawrence), p92 l (Gina Calvi), p92 r (Pictor International); Bridgeman Art Library/British Museum: p7; The Art Archive: p9 (Real Biblioteca de lo Escorial/Dagli Orti), p31 t (Monastery of Guadalupe Spain/Dagli Orti); Christine Osborne Pictures: p11; AKG-images: p12 (Stefan Diller), p13 (S.Domingie), p15, p17, p45 t (Glasgow Art Galleries and Museums: The St. Mungo Museum of Religious Life and Art), p136, p68; Sonia Halliday: p16, p60, p93 b (F.H.C. Birch); Corbis: p20 (Dave Bartruff); p25 (Gianni Dagli Orti), p29, p43 and p122 b (Richard T. Nowitz), p31 l (Francis G. Mayer), p30 t (Archivo Iconografico, S.A.), p37 r (Stephanie Maze), p55 (Elio Ciol), p67 (Michael S. Yamashita), p77 (Leif Skoogfors), p82 (Hanan Isachar), p84 (Annie Griffiths Belt), p88 (David Dixon; Papilio), p93 t (Angelo Hornak), p94 (Nik Wheeler), p95 (Richard Cummins), p96 (Kelly-Mooney Photography), p100, 126 and 147 (Bettmann), p106 (Ted Spiegel), p114 (Pablo Corral V), p122 t (Chris Lisle), p149 r (Underwood & Underwood), p152 bl (Wayside Madonna by Edith Catlin Phelps © Bowers Museum of Cultural Art); PA Photos: p31 br and p64 (EPA), p139, p41 r, p42, p150 l (Johnny Green); Circa Photo Library: p35, p37 l, p51 and p102 t (John Fryer), p130, p152 tr (Martin Palmer); Sonia Halliday and Laura Lushington: p39, p152 mr; AKG Photo: p41 l (Piero Baguzzi); Popperfoto/Michael Dalder/Reuters: p44; Scala, Florence: p45; CARTAGO FILMS/RAI/ITC/SIR LEW GRADE/Cortesía Album: p46; Reproduced with kind permission Kings College, Cambridge: p47; Simon Warner: p70, p97; Mary Evans Picture Library: p71, p129, p150 r; Reproduced with kind permission Salvation Army: p72; Reproduced with kind permission World Council Churches: p74; AP: p98 b (Hussein Malla), p102 b (Matt York), p108 t (John Moore); Impact Photos: p98 t (Mohamed Ansari); Rex Features: p99 (Simon Roberts); Reproduced with kind permission: p110; Topham Picturepoint: p115; ©BBC: p144, p146; James Hawkins Photography: p149 l; Ronald Grant Archive: p153; Reproduced with kind permission Christian Aid: p155.

The publishers would also like to thank the following for permission to reproduce material in this book:

Penguin and the Estate of Nevill Coghill for quotation of The Canterbury Tales by Geoffrey Chaucer, translated by Nevill Coghill, ©1951.

Every effort has been made to trace and acknowledge ownership of copyright. The publishers will be glad to make suitable arrangements with any copyright holders whom it has not been possible to contact.

Note about the Internet links in the book. The user should be aware that URLs or web addresses change regularly. Every effort has been made to ensure the accuracy of the URLs provided in this book on going to press. It is inevitable, however, that some will change. It is sometimes possible to find a relocated web page, by just typing in the address of the home page for a website in the URL window of your browser.

Orders: please contact Bookpoint Ltd, 130 Milton Park, Abingdon, Oxon OX14 4SB. Telephone: (44) 01235 827720. Fax: (44) 01235 400454. Lines are open from 9.00–6.00, Monday to Saturday, with a 24 hour message answering service. You can also order through our website www.hodderheadline.co.uk.

British Library Cataloguing in Publication Data
A catalogue record for this title is available from the British Library

ISBN 0 340 789 62 X

First Published 2003
Impression number   10 9 8 7 6 5 4 3 2 1
Year   2009 2008 2007 2006 2005 2004 2003

Copyright © Janet Green, Jon Mayled 2003

Typeset by Fakenham Photosetting Limited, Fakenham, Norfolk.
Printed in Italy for Hodder & Stoughton Educational, a division of Hodder Headline Ltd, 338 Euston Road, London NW1 3BH

CONTENTS

INTRODUCTION

Christianity is estimated to be the largest religion in the modern world and to have over 2020 million followers. Christianity, like Judaism and Islam, originated in the Middle East and is a monotheistic religion. This means the followers of the religion believe in one God.

The word 'Christianity' means that the believers commit themselves to following the Christ, which is the title they give to Jesus of Nazareth who lived two thousand years ago. The followers of Christianity are called Christians.

Christianity is a way of life as well as a religion. Beliefs are intended to affect behaviour and behaviour is expected to reflect beliefs.

It is important also to realise that different groups in a religion may emphasise varied aspects of the faith and that individual believers may be at different stages of spiritual growth and awareness. Most religions include a range of people; from nominal members, without any real sense of commitment, to devout followers who make their beliefs the focus of their lives. That is why it is important to try to avoid stereotypes and generalisations.

- What do you already know about Christianity? Work alone for a few minutes then in twos or threes. Compare your notes. Check for possible stereotypes and generalisations. Look again at your notes later in the course and see if your opinions have changed.

- Start a folder labelled 'Christianity: A Way of Life' for collecting material from the media about Christians.

- Make a note to remind yourself to put BCE (Before the Common Era) or CE (Common Era) after all historical dates. For centuries Christians wrote AD before stating the year in which an event happened. AD means Anno Domini in Latin. It means 'in the year of our Lord'. Nowadays we know they had not managed to work out exactly the real date for the birth of Jesus but it showed that to Christians this was the most significant event in history. When archaeologists began to find ancient artefacts, which dated before the time of Jesus, they used the abbreviation BC to show that the time was 'Before Christ'.

THINKING POINT

Imagine an alien has landed on Planet Earth. The alien happens to have beamed down into a country that considers itself to have a Christian heritage. Suggest the descriptions the alien might give about the beliefs and practices of Christianity.

BELIEFS

Roman rule at the time of Jesus.

THE BELIEFS OF CHRISTIANS

Christians are followers of Christ, which is a title used by them to refer to Jesus of Nazareth.

Historians usually accept that Jesus of Nazareth was a Palestinian Jew who lived two thousand years ago at a time when the Romans were the rulers of Palestine and of many other countries around the Mediterranean. Jesus was a preacher, teacher and healer but he made powerful enemies. He was crucified in about 30 CE in Jerusalem. There are non-Christian sources that refer to him and his followers.

JESUS IN WRITINGS BY NON-CHRISTIANS

Tacitus – a Roman historian who lived from about 58–116 CE.

Tacitus described the persecution of Christians by the Emperor Nero who blamed the Christian sect for the great fire in Rome in AD 64. Explaining who Christians were, Tacitus wrote that the originator of the name, Christus, had been executed when Tiberius was Emperor, by order of the procurator Pontius Pilate.

Suetonius – lived from 75–140 CE and was private secretary to Hadrian, the Roman Emperor.

Suetonius wrote books about the lives of the Caesars. In his book on Claudius he says the Emperor expelled Jews from Rome in 49 CE because 'the Jews constantly made disturbances at the instigation of Chrestus'. Suetonius is probably referring to an outbreak of quarrels between Jews and Christians. Many early Christians were Jews and the dispute would look to outsiders like a quarrel among Jews. Scholars think the text shows, however, that Suetonius assumed there had been a historical figure called 'Chrestus'.

Pliny – governor of part of what is now Turkey, writing in 112 CE.

Pliny wrote a letter to the Emperor Trajan to ask advice about the way to deal with people who had been accused of being Christians. Pliny writes:

'The people who had once been Christians told me that their 'crime' amounted to this – they met on a set day to sing hymns to Christ as a god and to swear an oath together. This was not with the aim of committing crimes but to refrain from theft, adultery, lying and not paying one's debts. They ate an ordinary meal together. They claimed that they had stopped this after I banned societies from meeting. To be sure about this I decided to get at the truth by torturing two slave girls called deaconesses. I found nothing but a perverse and weird superstition.'

Flavius Josephus – a Jewish soldier who was taken prisoner and became a friend of the Emperor Vespasian. He lived from about 37 CE to the end of the first century.

Josephus settled in Rome and wrote about Jewish history for the Romans. He referred to Jesus but it is difficult to be sure whether or not some of the comments have been added by later Christian writers. One reference usually accepted by scholars is about a High Priest called Ananus who assembled the Sanhedrin Council 'and brought before them James, the brother of Jesus who was called the Christ, and some others'.

Do you think Jesus looked like this?

To find the beliefs that Christians have about Jesus, one needs to look at Christian sources, particularly a collection of writings called the New Testament. To Christians, these writings are a continuation of the Jewish Scriptures, which they call the Old Testament. Together, the Old Testament and the New Testament make the Christian Bible. (Testament means covenant or agreement; see Chapter 7.) The New Testament includes stories about Jesus and letters by Christian leaders. Most of it was originally written in Greek, the language most commonly used in the Mediterranean area at the time.

When Christianity began the leaders were people who had known Jesus. The followers were mostly Jews, by race and religion. They were known as followers of 'The Way' and they were a sect within Judaism. When new members joined the movement they were baptised in water, usually in a river, and they simply acknowledged that they wanted to follow Jesus. They were not stating what they believed so much as expressing their loyalty to their leader.

THINKING POINT

Look at the description in Pliny's letter of the activities of Christians. Try to imagine those first Christians. What do you think the 'oath' was?

One of the earliest statements of commitment seems to have been 'Jesus Christ is Lord'.

The word 'Christ' in Greek stands for the word 'Messiah' in Hebrew. To the Jews the word 'Messiah' referred to a leader whose coming had been prophesied in the Jewish Scriptures. Messiah means 'Anointed One'. Kings, prophets and priests were anointed in the Jewish religion. Most Jews did not accept the claim that Jesus was the expected Messiah and the Roman authorities saw the claim as treason. When Jesus was crucified in Jerusalem, the accusation over the cross read 'Jesus of Nazareth, King of the Jews'.

The word 'Lord' (κυριος in Greek) was significant to both Jews and non-Jews. 'Lord' was the word used for the sacred name of God in translations of the Jewish Scriptures but it was used also of the Roman Emperor. Before long, there would be many who would pay with their lives for daring to offer their loyalty first to Jesus as Christ and Lord.

The word 'disciple' comes from the Latin *disco* 'I learn' but the disciples of Jesus were not risking their lives simply because they wanted to continue to learn from his teachings. The main reason that the followers of Jesus accepted their crucified leader as their Lord was that they believed that Jesus rose from the dead after his crucifixion. The New Testament describes him being seen by a number of different people during the next 40 days. Among the witnesses of the Resurrection were the apostles. These were disciples who had been chosen by Jesus during his ministry to be 'sent out' to spread his message, which was the gospel or good news about the Kingdom of God.

Jesus promised, before finally leaving them, that they would receive the power of the Holy Spirit to spread the message throughout the world.

The adventures of the apostles are told in the New Testament book, the Acts of the Apostles. The message they preached is included so we have some idea of the beliefs they were spreading. In the first sermon that the Apostle Peter gives in Jerusalem, according to the account in Acts 2, he says:

> *God has raised this Jesus to life, and we are all witnesses of the fact . . . God has made this Jesus, whom you crucified, both Lord and Christ.*
>
> (Acts 2:32 and 36b)

The letters in the New Testament written by Christian leaders also demonstrate the beliefs they were spreading:

> *For what I received I passed on to you as of first importance: that Christ died for our sins according to the Scriptures, that he was buried, that he was raised on the third day according to the Scriptures, and that he appeared to Peter, and then to the Twelve. After that, he appeared to more than five hundred of the brothers at the same time, most of whom are still living, though some have fallen asleep.*
>
> (The missionary Paul writing to the church at Corinth in 1 Corinthians 15:3–6)

The word 'church' (ecclesia in Greek) did not mean a building. It was the word used for all the people who were followers of Jesus. The movement grew fast and spread rapidly through the Roman Empire. It became so popular among non-Jews (Gentiles) that they soon outnumbered the Jewish Christians. Many slaves became Christians too.

Statements of belief are called creeds, from the Latin word 'Credo' which means 'I believe'. The creeds were carefully worded because they were intended to stop mistaken ideas called 'heresies' from developing. Many heresies were trying to answer questions that still puzzle Christians today, such as 'How can Jesus be both God and man?' The creeds do not seek to answer all the questions. They simply list the beliefs that were passed down from the time of the Apostles.

There is a legend that the 12 Apostles wrote a creed. Each apostle supposedly wrote one sentence of it. We know that there was an accepted 'rule of faith' circulating in the second century among Christian churches which seems to have been some sort of credal statement.

One creed accepted by most Christian Churches is called the Apostles' Creed. It probably dates back to the fourth century CE though it is likely that it is based on earlier creeds.

Reciting a creed is a reminder of the key beliefs which have been passed down by the Church.

THE APOSTLES' CREED

I believe in God, the Father almighty, creator of heaven and Earth.

I believe in Jesus Christ, his only Son, our Lord.

He was conceived by the power of the Holy Spirit and born of the Virgin Mary.

He suffered under Pontius Pilate, was crucified, died and was buried.

He descended to the dead.

On the third day he rose again.

He ascended into heaven, and is seated at the right hand of the Father.

He will come again to judge the living and the dead.

I believe in the Holy Spirit, the holy Catholic Church, the communion of saints, the forgiveness of sins, the resurrection of the body, and the life everlasting. Amen.

THE TRINITY

The Apostles' Creed expresses Christian beliefs about the Trinity – Father, Son and Holy Spirit.

The Trinity is central to Christian belief and is a teaching which makes Christianity different from all other religions. People outside Christianity sometimes think that Christians believe in three gods but this is not so.

Christianity is a monotheistic religion which has one God. The Trinity is a way of describing belief in three aspects of God which believers experience. The one God is made up of three persons: God the Father, God the Son and God the Holy Spirit.

THREE IN ONE AND ONE IN THREE

Tertullian, a Roman second-century Christian writer, described the Trinity as the sun sending out rays of sunshine.

Father

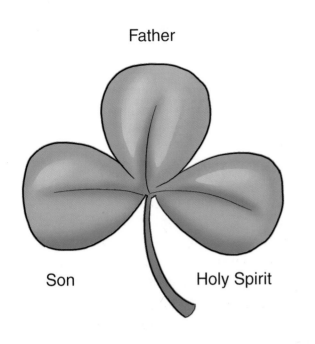

Son   Holy Spirit

A legend says that St Patrick used a shamrock as a visual aid. Just like a shamrock has three parts in one leaf, so God is three parts in one being.

This is a mediaeval drawing to show the Trinity.

NICENE CREED

There are other creeds used by Christians today, besides the Apostles' Creed, for example, the Nicene Creed. This was created after the Emperor Constantine made Christianity the official religion of the Roman Empire. He called a council of Christian leaders and they met at Nicaea (Isnik in modern Turkey) in 325 CE. The Nicene Creed expands the same beliefs which are outlined in the Apostles' Creed. The council was called to consider the teaching of a theologian called Arius. He taught that Jesus did not possess the nature of God but only that of man. The council rejected his teaching as heresy.

We believe in one God,
the Father, the Almighty, maker of heaven and earth,
of all that is, seen and unseen. We believe in one
Lord, Jesus Christ, the only Son of God, eternally
begotten of the Father, God from God, Light from
Light, true God from true God, begotten, not made,
of one Being with the Father.
Through him all things were made. For us men and
for our salvation he came down from heaven: by the
power of the Holy Spirit he became incarnate from
the Virgin Mary, and was made man.
For our sake he was crucified under Pontius Pilate; he

suffered death and was buried. On the third day he rose again in accordance with the Scriptures; he ascended into heaven and is seated at the right hand of the Father.

He will come again in glory to judge the living and the dead, and his kingdom will have no end.

We believe in the Holy Spirit, the Lord, the giver of life, who proceeds from the Father and the Son.

With the Father and the Son, he is worshipped and glorified.

He has spoken through the Prophets.

We believe in one holy catholic and apostolic Church.

We acknowledge one baptism for the forgiveness of sins. We look for the resurrection of the dead, and the life of the world to come. Amen.

FATHER

'I believe in God the Father Almighty, maker of heaven and earth.'

There are some people who do not believe in the existence of God or gods but for most religious people belief in a creator is the starting point of their faith.

People wonder about the answers to questions, such as 'How did the world begin?', 'Why are we here?' and 'What is life all about?' Science provides some answers but these ultimate questions also provoke religious responses. You cannot expect to prove beliefs in the way in which you might check a mathematical fact or a scientific formula. Beliefs are a matter of faith.

'In the beginning God created the heavens and the earth.'

The Apostles' Creed echoes these words which are found in Genesis 1:1 at the start of the Bible. The existence of God was taken for granted.

Christians reciting the Apostles' Creed begin with the same assumption. They accept that God is the ground of our being, the First Cause, the reason behind the existence of everything. They believe that God is the designer and creator of the universe. This is the same God who is written about in both the Old Testament and the New Testament. This is the same God that Jesus prayed to as Father.

Not only did God the Father create the universe but he sustains it. He continues to rule and control everything. God is almighty. He is omnipotent; having the power to do anything. He is omniscient; knowing everything. He is omnipresent; God is everywhere. No one can hide from God.

THINKING POINT

Theologians talk of the transcendence of God. By this they mean all the characteristics which portray God as mysterious and beyond human comprehension, imagination and explanation. God's supreme greatness, holiness and transcendence commands the response, from humans, of awe, worship, fear, wonder and respect. Even the word 'God' is beyond definition.

Can you think of any descriptions of God in Christian hymns which can add to this idea of the transcendence of the almighty Creator God?

Some religious people would never try to paint a picture of God. What do you think are their reasons?

It is natural to want to know about the character or nature of God. If there is one God who created the universe, what is this one God like? Is God really so distant and so remote that we can never know?

It is important to Christians that God is identified as Father even before acknowledging him as creator. Jesus taught his disciples to begin their prayers with the words 'Our Father'. Jesus taught that God cares about everything and everybody; that God the Father is a loving Father, who is kind and merciful but also just and fair. Christians affirm that we can know these things because God has revealed himself to humans in many ways and continues to do so.

One way God reveals himself is in the world which he created. Christians believe not only in the transcendence of God but also in the immanence of God. This means that he is close to and cares for even the smallest part of his creation. Christians believe that the natural world can point people towards God. Of course, people need to be in a sensitive and receptive frame of mind to be able to see the spiritual dimension in the physical, material world.

To see a World in a Grain of Sand,
And a Heaven in a Wild Flower,
Hold Infinity in the palm of your hand,
And Eternity in an hour.

(*Auguries of Innocence*, William Blake (1757–1827))

God also reveals himself through the holy book, the Bible, through the Christian church and through the individual conscience. Both the Old Testament and the New Testament are full of accounts of God communicating with individuals in all sorts of ways. Christians believe that God continues to do this. The Bible itself is called the Word of God by many Christians and they study it to obtain guidance from God in their daily life.

Most important of all for Christians is the belief that God revealed himself in his Son.

FOR DISCUSSION

Read the account of the creation in Genesis 1:1–2:3. Thousands of years old, it was originally written in Hebrew verse and was probably used in processions and ceremonies at the start of the Jewish year. What ideas is it expressing? How far does it fit with scientific ideas?

Some Christians feel uneasy that Christianity uses patriarchal masculine language so much. What do you feel about the suggestion that God should be called Mother rather than Father?

Keeping in mind Christian beliefs about God, suggest global issues which you think Christians might be concerned about and explain why.

SON
IXTOS

I	Iesous	Jesus
C	Christos	Christ
TH	Theou	of God
U	Uios	Son
S	Soter	Saviour

Some historians think Christians may have hidden in the catacombs under Rome during persecution. It is certain that the Christians buried their dead in the tunnels because archaeological remains have been found there. These include inscriptions. Some use secret signs which were necessary at the time. It was dangerous to be a Christian.

The cross is an obvious symbol for Christians. Another symbol they use is a fish. The sign of the fish is appropriate for followers of Jesus whose first disciples were fishermen but it signifies far more. It is in fact an acronym. Each letter is the initial of a word. The sentence expresses belief in Jesus Christ Son of God Saviour.

Another symbol is known as the Chi-Rho. These are the first two letters of Christ in Greek.

The Apostles' Creed gives Jesus the title 'Christ'. It is often treated as if it were his surname.

The belief that Jesus is the Christ (Messiah) runs throughout the New Testament. Both the Gospel of Matthew and the Gospel of Mark refer to him as Jesus Christ in their first verse. He is frequently

The Greek is pronounced Christos.

portrayed as the fulfilment of specific prophecies made in the Jewish Scriptures about the Messiah.

The next phrase about Jesus in the Apostles' Creed refers to him as God's 'only Son'. The Nicene Creed goes into more depth about this belief concerning Jesus Christ being the Son of God. It contains such phrases as 'eternally begotten of the Father, true God from true God, begotten not made, of one Being with the Father'. Many Christians find it helpful to meditate on these phrases.

To Gentile Christians, the words 'Son of God' may not have been a very staggering idea. They were used to emperors and heroes being dubbed son of this god or that god in a system which was polytheistic. They needed to acknowledge Jesus as the ONLY Son of God.

Christians believe that, by some miracle or by some mystery, Jesus of Nazareth was God incarnate. This means God was in Jesus in a very special way. God became flesh and blood. For Christians, the doctrine of the incarnation means that the theological idea of the immanence of God takes on a whole new dimension. God really does know what it is like to be human.

'Our Lord' is the next title in the Apostles' Creed. At the time when it was written, the word 'Lord' meant far more to Jews and to Roman citizens than it means nowadays but this title remains the key statement in all Christian creeds. It is not simply a matter of saying that Jesus is Lord but being willing to live a life which shows that Jesus is Lord.

'Go forth to love and serve the Lord' is what Christianity has always been about.

Christians accept Jesus as Lord because, to them, Jesus is the perfect example and they try to follow him.

The Birth of Christ by Giotto di Bondone.

The Apostles' Creed starts with the birth. On the one hand, Jesus is God's Son, conceived by the power of the Holy Spirit, not by normal sexual intercourse. On the other hand, Jesus was born from a human mother named Mary. According to the creed, she was a virgin.

For many Christians, Mary is very important. Some Christians, however, have found the Virgin Birth to be a belief that they feel they cannot take literally.

A TEXTUAL DEBATE

Matthew 1:23 (NIV) quotes from the Jewish Scriptures 'The virgin will be with child and will give birth to a son, and they will call him Immanuel', which means 'God with us'.

Matthew liked to use Old Testament texts to support Christian beliefs about Jesus as Messiah. Matthew was quoting from the Greek version of Isaiah 7:14 but in the Hebrew original the word simply means a young woman, not necessarily a virgin. Some scholars think this is how the doctrine of the virgin birth started. Others point out, however, that it is not only in Matthew's gospel. The Virgin Birth is a main feature in the nativity story in Luke's gospel too.

The creed moves to the end of the life of Jesus. Pontius Pilate, the Roman Governor in Jerusalem from 26–36 CE who judged Jesus and ordered that he should be crucified, is named in the Apostles' Creed.

The suffering, crucifixion, death and burial are important items in the creed. There was a popular heresy in the early church which said that Jesus was divine so he could not and did not die on the cross. Some people even suggested that Simon of Cyrene who helped carry the cross was crucified in the place of Jesus. To Christians the crucifixion of Jesus is very important because they believe that Jesus died to make it possible for people's sins to be forgiven. All people fall short of God's standards and the result is separation from God. The New Testament teaches that the death of Jesus was part of God's plan for reconciling the world to himself. Christians believe that Jesus Christ took the punishment for the sins of the whole world so that God and humanity could be made as one. This teaching is called the Atonement.

The Apostles' Creed says that Jesus descended to the dead. The reason it uses the word 'descended' is because people at the time thought that the world was flat. Heaven was up above the earth and there was a place below the earth where the dead waited till the end of time. It was called 'Sheol' by Jews and 'Hades' by Greeks.

Crucifixion of Christ by Fra Giovanni da Fiesole.

> *For Christ died for sins once for all, the righteous for the unrighteous, to bring you to God. He was put to death in the body but made alive by the Spirit, through whom also he went and preached to the spirits in prison who disobeyed long ago when God waited patiently in the days of Noah while the ark was being built.*
>
> (1 Peter 3:18–20)

The word 'prison' in this passage is believed to refer to Hell.

The Resurrection has always been central to the Christian message. For Christians, the resurrection proves that Jesus is the promised Messiah and that there is life after death. Easter is the festival when Christians celebrate the Resurrection but it is celebrated every Sunday and at every Eucharist. 'The third day' was actually a Sunday. It was the first day of the week. The believers in the resurrected Jesus began holding meetings on the first day as well as attending the Jewish synagogue on Saturdays. Soon it became one of the ways of identifying Christians. When Christianity was outlawed, the fact that people met on Sunday was evidence against them.

The resurrected Jesus was not a ghost. He was so real that the disciples ate and drank with him. The New Testament recounts various resurrection appearances which occurred during the next 40 days. Then Jesus appeared for one last time before he returned to his Father in the mystery of the Ascension. The Acts of the Apostles gives a description of the Ascension of Jesus (Acts 1:1–11). Christians still visit the place where this is said to have happened on the Mount of Olives outside the walls of Jerusalem. The Apostles' Creed is expressing the conviction that Jesus returned to be with God and is in the place of highest honour, 'seated at the right hand'.

The belief that Jesus will come again to judge the living and the dead is part of eschatology, the study of the last things. The word 'apocalyptic' comes from a Greek word meaning to uncover or reveal. It implies a dramatic event when God breaks into history. The belief that God created and controls the universe leads to the inevitable conclusion that God will be in control of the end of the world. The return of Christ is called the Parousia, the Appearing. This dramatic event will automatically bring Judgement because no longer will there be the opportunity to choose to believe.

HOLY SPIRIT

According to Acts 1, before the Ascension of Jesus, he promised that his disciples would receive the power of the Holy Spirit. The word for power in Greek is 'dunamis'. We get the word 'dynamite' from it. Acts goes on to tell, in chapter 2, how on the Day of Pentecost the Holy Spirit fell on the followers of Jesus. The experience had such an amazing impact that their lives were totally changed. Christians celebrate the giving of the Holy Spirit at Whitsuntide. It is regarded as the birthday of the Christian Church.

Christians believe that the Holy Spirit continues to work in the world. In John's gospel Jesus calls the Holy Spirit the paraclete which is a Greek word for 'the Comforter'. Christians believe that the Holy Spirit gives them guidance, faith, hope, understanding and the spiritual strength to live up to the teachings of Jesus. The power of the Holy Spirit, they believe, is what inspires people and gives special charismatic gifts, such as the ability to preach, teach, heal, prophesy and speak in tongues like the disciples did after Pentecost. Most important of all, the Holy Spirit helps them to spread love in the world.

> *But the fruit of the Spirit is love, joy, peace, patience, kindness, goodness, faithfulness, gentleness and self-control.*
>
> (Galatians 5:22–32a)

Christians believe that the Holy Spirit has always been at work in the world. The Holy Spirit referred to in the Apostles' Creed is the same Spirit of God which hovered over the waters at creation and the same Spirit which spoke the word of God through the Old Testament Prophets. The word for spirit in Hebrew is 'ruach'. It can also be translated as breath or wind.

The Nicene Creed says that the Holy Spirit proceeds from the Father and the Son ('Filioque' is the word for 'and the Son' in Latin). Some Christians wanted to leave out 'filioque' because they felt that it implied that the Holy Spirit was less important than the first two persons of the Trinity. In fact, this was one of the points which led to the split between the Christians in the West and those in the East in 1054 (see page 63).

The next statements in the Apostles' Creed are all part of the Holy Spirit working through the church. The Holy Catholic Church refers to the universal church. The word 'Catholic' comes from the Greek word 'Katholikos' meaning universal.

The communion of saints means the fellowship which unites all Christians.

The forgiveness of sins is a process which Christians experience by the prompting of the Holy Spirit. It starts with recognising that something is a sin, seeing the need to repent and being truly sorry. Then, believing the promise that God will forgive sins, the Christian can confess the sin, stop feeling guilty and make a new start in the power of the Holy Spirit.

In the phrase 'resurrection of the body' the creed reflects the Jewish background from which Christianity grew.

The Jews did not believe in an immortal soul in the way that many Greeks did. In Genesis 2:7 when God creates Adam, he breathes into him and Adam becomes a living being. The word in Hebrew for this living being is 'nephesh' which means both body and soul; the physical and the spiritual together. The Jews believed that each living being has one life and then dies. The Jewish Scriptures do not contain much teaching about what happens after death. But a belief developed that at the Last Day the dead would rise for Judgement. To the present day, many Jews, Christians and Muslims bury their dead rather than cremating them because of the belief in the resurrection of the body.

The Resurrection by Sir Stanley Spencer.

The creed is expressing the Christian belief that death is not the end. Most Christians are content to accept the teaching in I Corinthians 15 where the resurrection of the body is described as a transformation and a mystery.

The word 'Amen' simply means 'So be it'. It is a Hebrew word expressing the certainty that something is true.

FOR DISCUSSION

Can you think of any examples which might count as 'sins of omission'?

Look up the following references to see what Jesus is said to have included in 'sins of omission': Matthew 22:23 and Matthew 25:31–45.

SIN, JUDGEMENT, FORGIVENESS, SALVATION, ETERNAL LIFE

SIN

A word used in the New Testament for sin is hamartia – missing the mark.

Sin is disobedience against the will of God, falling short of God's standards and falling away from the perfection of God.

Thoughts, words and actions which result from 'sin' are called 'sins'. People who commit sins are called 'sinners'.

Sometimes sins include actions which have not been done. These are 'sins of omission'. They have not been done but they should have been done.

Adam and Eve being cast out of the Garden of Eden. 1887 Window by Lorin in St. Aignan Church, Chartres.

The story of Adam and Eve in Genesis 3 is about the first sin. It presents the idea that, from the very beginning when God first created them and gave them free will, human beings have been rebellious and disobedient. The idea that all people are born in a state of sin with a natural inclination to do wrong is called 'original sin'. This is a Christian idea and although the Old Testament is a Jewish book, Jews do not believe in original sin.

Christians have different ideas about original sin. Some see it as a sort of stain which is passed on and on from parents to children, and some see it as guilt handed down from the time of Adam, whilst others simply accept that original sin is a way of expressing the fact that human nature is weak.

In the Bible, in both the Old Testament and the New Testament, sin is shown to separate people from God. Baptism of children and adults is seen by Christians as one of the ways of washing away sin and sins in order to start a new life filled with the power of the Holy Spirit (see page 113).

JUDGEMENT

Belief in judgement has always been part of Christian teaching. Both the Old Testament and the New Testament say that God is just; sin is wrong and, therefore, sin should be punished.

Christians believe that this life is a preparation for the next life, life after death. By words like 'the next life' and 'the afterlife', Christians do not mean reincarnation. Christians believe that we have only this one life on earth and in it we are tested; then we are rewarded or punished. Believers will go to Heaven. Heaven is where God is. Sinners will be separated from God. They will be in Hell. Roman Catholics believe there is a state of existence called Purgatory where people who deserve some punishment or are not fully prepared for heaven will go to be cleansed and made ready to meet God.

Many Christians believe that there will be an actual 'Day of Judgement' at the end of time when the world ends.

In the Old Testament book of Daniel there is a prophecy of 'one like a human being' coming in the sky (Daniel 7:13). This is often translated as 'one like a son of man'. Jesus used the title 'Son of Man' and the Gospel writers saw it as a Messianic title. From New Testament times, Christians have awaited this Second Coming of Jesus. The Creeds also refer to the return of Christ and the final Judgement (see above).

Some Christians accept the biblical prophecies about the events at the end of the world as a literal account of what will happen, whilst others see the descriptions as picture language to express faith in the final triumph of God's kingdom over all evil.

In medieval times Christian churches often had lurid paintings of the Last Judgement with the believers in Heaven with God and the damned souls being tortured and tormented in the fires of Hell.

FOR DISCUSSION

Christian preachers often point to the fact that the word 'sin' has the letter 'i' in the middle. They say that this reminds us that putting 'I', one's own self, as the centre of one's life will always lead to unhappiness. Do you agree?

Look at the Ten Commandments (see page 21). Breaking any one of these commandments shows the sort of behaviour which might be called sinful. Do you think everybody breaks these rules?

The Last Judgement by Jean Cousin the Younger.

In the New Testament, Hell is sometimes called Gehenna. This was a reference to the Valley of Hinnom, a rubbish dump outside Jerusalem where the rubbish was burnt. The fires never went out and it made a vivid metaphor for a place of eternal punishment.

To Christians, one thing is certain about the afterlife; it lasts forever. It is not surprising therefore that belief in an afterlife can influence the behaviour of believers in their present life.

FOR DISCUSSION

How might belief in a Day of Judgement and life after death affect the attitudes and behaviour of believers? Try to think of both positive and negative effects.

The fact that every individual is responsible for his or her actions implies another important belief: that humans have been created with free will. Christians believe that people are free to choose to follow the teachings of Christianity or to reject them but they must face the consequences of their decision at the Last Judgement. At first it seems difficult to reconcile the idea of free will with the complete control that God has over everything. Christians have different beliefs about predestination and free will and the balance between the two. Sometimes the idea of predestination is described as being like a game of chess. The players can see the moves as the game progresses and they can think ahead to some of the strategies to deal with the possibilities. A chess master can see further ahead than most people and predict the outcome of the game. God is omniscient, he knows everything. God has no restrictions and can see both past and future. The players have their freedom to make their moves in the game of life but the plans of God anticipate and incorporate what he knows is going to happen. This is Predestination by Foreknowledge. God is also more caring than we can imagine. Christians trust God to know best and to do what is best for them.

Christians believe that God is omnipotent; that means God has the power to do anything. Nothing is impossible with God. Obviously this raises some other important religious questions. If God is so powerful and cares so much then how does Christianity explain the existence of evil and suffering?

Christians believe that God's creation was perfect. This creation included other unseen worlds besides the physical natural universe and other beings besides humans and animals. Among these beings are angels, messengers of God, who have no free will and no physical bodies, though they can take on human shape.

Many Christians believe that a fallen angel, 'Lucifer, Son of the Morning', was cast out of heaven but is allowed to tempt humans till the Day of Judgement. This tempter is known as Satan or the Devil. The gospels tell of Jesus being tempted by the Devil in the wilderness.

The Biblical explanation of evil points to a very important conviction: that, however bad things may seem in the world, good is more powerful than evil. It is not a battle between two equal forces or two gods. There is only One God. In the end, good is certain to win. In fact, according to Christians the main victory has been won already, when Jesus was crucified and rose again.

FORGIVENESS

Jesus taught his followers to pray to God for forgiveness for their sins. The first step towards forgiveness is repentance. This means being truly sorry for the things you have done which are wrong. It also means trying to make amends for the wrongdoing.

The need for repentance and confession is mentioned often in the Jewish Scriptures, especially by the prophets.

Jesus himself used to forgive sins. On the cross he even forgave his enemies.

Father, forgive them, for they do not know what they are doing.

(Luke 23:34)

Jesus taught his followers that if they were truly repentant then God would forgive them, no matter what dreadful things they had done. They could stop feeling guilty and get on with living a new life.

For some Christians the experience of knowing that they are forgiven is so emotional and overpowering that they describe it as feeling like the burden of sin has fallen from their back.

Christian losing his burden at the cross, from John Bunyan's 'Pilgrim's Progress'.

Though Christians can confess their sins and pray to God at home, some prefer to confess their sins to a priest in confidence. The power 'to loose and bind' (to forgive sins) was given to the apostles (according to Matthew 16:19 and 18:18) and in some churches priests have the authority to give absolution, to say that the sins are forgiven.

Many Christian churches organise their services to include a general confession spoken by the whole congregation followed by absolution in the communion service.

Christians believe that they cannot buy forgiveness and they cannot earn forgiveness by doing good deeds. They believe that if they have faith that Jesus died for their sins they will be forgiven by the free grace of God.

At the Last Supper when Jesus offered the cup of wine to his disciples, he said, 'This is my blood of the covenant, which is poured out for many for the forgiveness of sins.' Christians remember these words when they celebrate the Eucharist (see page 97).

If Christians appreciate the fact that their sins are forgiven then they will show their gratitude and be generous in forgiving other people.

Be kind and compassionate to one another, forgiving each other, just as in Christ God forgave you.

(Ephesians 4:32)

Roman Catholics distinguish between mortal sins which are serious matters (e.g. murder) and venial sins which are the failings of everyday life. Mortal sins need to be confessed to a priest.

From very early times, priests were meant to keep secret what they were told in the confessional and it has been a church law ever since 1215.

SALVATION

Jesus Christ . . . who for us men and for our salvation came down from heaven. (Nicene Creed)

Salvation is the healing of a broken relationship between people and God, which brings new life and peace.

When they experience forgiveness of sin and commit themselves to following Jesus, some Christians say that they have been saved. They are using the language of the New Testament.

In the New Testament, Jesus is described as 'the Saviour of the world' (1 John 4:14). Christians believe that Jesus saves people from their sins. In John's gospel Jesus is called 'the Lamb of God who takes away the sin of the world' (John 1:29).

In Mark 10:45 Jesus says, 'For even the Son of Man did not come to be served, but to serve, and to give his life as a ransom for many.'

Salvation is also called redemption and another Christian title for Jesus Christ is the Redeemer. This idea comes from the practice of buying back, redeeming or paying the price for a slave's freedom.

Many of the metaphors to explain how Jesus paid for human sin continue to be used by Christians today. The situation is sometimes likened to a court room in which justice had to be done. Jesus accepted the penalty which was due as the punishment for sin even though he had done no wrong. He died in the place of sinners. He atoned for what they had done wrong.

Sometimes Christians talk about the blood of Jesus washing away sin. They are describing the crucifixion as a sacrifice of the life-blood, a pure offering which had to be made to appease a just God for the sins of the world.

This makes God seem harsh but Christians say God was providing a solution to the problem of sin because of his love for humankind.

Christians had a rich heritage of Jewish ideas to draw from. Jesus and his followers were always quoting the Jewish Scriptures. Atonement was a familiar idea to them because of Yom Kippur, the Day of Atonement, which is a fasting day on the tenth day after Rosh Hashanah, the New Year.

A goat, a scapegoat, used to be driven into the wilderness symbolically carrying away the sins of the people.

Jewish rituals at this time involve confessing sins and making a new start. To atone means to make up for something which was wrong. On the Day of Atonement, sins are atoned for and God and the people are reconciled, they are made as one.

Christians borrowed this idea to express their belief that the death of Jesus was for all time the atonement for the sin of the world.

> *He is the atoning sacrifice for our sins, and not only for ours but also for the sins of the whole world.*
>
> (1 John 2:2)

ETERNAL LIFE

When people die who believe in God they are said to be in a state of grace and Christians believe their souls will go to heaven and have eternal life. God is eternal so friendship with God is eternal.

Life after death is sometimes called everlasting life. This is because it goes on for ever. Unbelievers are said to spend forever in hell. Christians have different ideas about hell. The New Testament pictures it as flames but also as weeping and gnashing of teeth in outer darkness, which is a way of describing unhappiness at being separated from God.

> *For God so loved the world that he gave his one and only Son, that whoever believes in him shall not perish but have eternal life.*
>
> (John 3:16)

In New Testament teaching, especially in the Gospel of John, the eternal life which is promised to believers is not simply everlasting life, something that goes on for ever. Eternal life with God refers not only to quantity, or length of time, but also to quality of life. Christians believe that eternal life with God is something so good and so beautiful that it is beyond human imagination but they can have a glimpse of it because in some ways eternal life, heaven and hell begin here on earth.

John's gospel says the moment of accepting the Christian faith is a new start, so it is like being born all over again. Eternal life for the believer has started at that moment.

THE TEN COMMANDMENTS

Then God spoke all these words. He said:

I am Yahweh your God who brought you out of Egypt, where you lived as slaves. 'You shall have no other gods to rival me. You shall not make yourself a carved image or any likeness of anything in heaven above or on earth beneath or in the waters under the earth. You shall not bow down to them or serve them. For I, Yahweh your God, am a jealous God and I punish a parent's fault in the children, the grandchildren, and the great-grandchildren among those who hate me; but I act with faithful love towards thousands of those who love me and keep my commandments. You shall not misuse the name of Yahweh your God, for Yahweh will not leave unpunished anyone who misuses his name. Remember the Sabbath day and keep it holy. For six days you shall labour and do all your work, but the seventh day is a Sabbath for Yahweh your God. You shall do no work that day, neither you nor your son nor your daughter nor your servants, men or women, nor your animals nor the alien living with you. For in six days Yahweh made the heavens, earth and sea and all that these contain, but on the seventh day he rested; that is why Yahweh has blessed the Sabbath day and made it sacred. Honour your father and your mother so that you may live long in the land that Yahweh your God is giving you. You shall not kill. You shall not commit adultery. You shall not steal. You shall not give false evidence against your neighbour. You shall not set your heart on your neighbour's house. You shall not set your heart on your neighbour's spouse, or servant, man or woman, or ox, or donkey, or any of your neighbour's possessions.

(Exodus 20:1–17 The New Jerusalem Bible)

The Ten Commandments are over three thousand years old. The original laws were written on stone and they were kept in the Ark of the Covenant which accompanied the Hebrew tribes on their wanderings through the wilderness.

The Hebrew slaves had escaped from Egypt and they entered into a covenant with God which was given through their leader, the prophet Moses, on Mount Sinai. The first five books of the Jewish Scriptures contain the Torah, the Law which was given to Moses and which the Hebrews promised to keep as their side of the agreement. The Ten Commandments (the Decalogue) are part of the Law.

The first four rules are about the way the people should behave towards God and the last six are about the behaviour of people to each other.

Jews try to keep these laws to the present day. Christians also show respect for these rules but, at the same time, they try to keep to the principles that Jesus explained when he was talking about these commandments in the Sermon on the Mount.

THINKING POINT

Check that you understand what all the words in the Ten Commandments mean.

Jews follow a lunar calendar. The day begins at sunset so the Jewish Sabbath begins on Friday sunset and finishes on Saturday sunset. Sabbath means resting day. Christians follow a solar calendar, so each day starts at 12 midnight and their holy day is Sunday but they treat it as their holy Sabbath (see page 53).

Why were the people expected to keep the Ten Commandments? Look again at the first commandment.

THE CHRISTIAN IDEAL

THE SERMON ON THE MOUNT, MATTHEW 5–7

Jesus was said to be a good teacher. It is unlikely that Jesus sat on a mountain and delivered these three chapters all at once.

THINKING POINT

These three chapters are a block of teaching. If you had such a collection to place in a book about Jesus how would you arrange them?

Would you:
• Scatter the sayings throughout the book?
• Try to place each one near a relevant incident?
• Put them all together in any order and let the reader sort it out?
• Keep them together but try to structure them so particular themes could be developed?

Think of the advantages and disadvantages in each case.

Matthew included the material near the beginning of the ministry of Jesus and set the scene on a mountain. Luke used the same collection of sayings but he set the sermon on a plain (Luke 6:7–49) and used 34 verses elsewhere in his gospel.

Matthew's gospel was written for Jewish Christians. They would be familiar with the idea of Moses being given the Law on Mount Sinai. Matthew had more sayings besides these. He put them in five blocks throughout the gospel. Sometimes the Sermon on the Mount is called the new law. Every time in this Sermon that Jesus says 'But I tell you' he is claiming special authority.

MATTHEW CHAPTER 5
Matthew 5:1–12

The sermon begins with the beatitudes which are a list of eight kinds of people who are blessed in God's eyes. (Beatitude is from the Latin for blessing.)

The blessed are not the people you would expect to describe as happy or contented. They are:

- The poor in spirit – the humble, those who know their need of God.
- Those who mourn – the sorrowful, the bereaved, the repentant.
- The meek – of a gentle disposition – not pushy, not proud, not arrogant.
- Those who hunger and thirst for righteousness, they want to do God's will.
- The merciful – those who show compassion, pity, love and forgiveness.
- The pure in heart – their religion is sincere; their motives are not selfish.
- The peacemakers – they work to solve conflict fairly between individuals and in society.
- Those who are persecuted because of righteousness; they suffer persecution for a righteous cause, not for their own wrongdoing.

The passage promises that 'Theirs is the Kingdom of Heaven' now, not only in the future, because people with spiritual values have a clear conscience and peace with God.

Two verses are added after the beatitudes which are more sayings of Jesus about persecution. At the time Matthew wrote the gospel the early church was suffering persecution and some Christians were facing death for their beliefs.

FOR DISCUSSION

Take two beatitudes and consider:
- exactly what they mean
- how Christians might put them into practice
- why each one might result in happiness (each beatitude has a promise attached).

Compare your ideas with those of other people.

Matthew 5:13–16

Christians are called the salt of the earth and the light of the world. Salt purifies, preserves and adds flavour; light drives away darkness and shines so people can see clearly.

These metaphors challenge Christians to show their faith in the world. If they are the sort of people described in the beatitudes they will do so; Christians are supposed to be an influence for good wherever they go and they are expected to spread the light of the gospel throughout the world.

Matthew 5:17–19

There is an incident later in the life of Jesus which is called the Transfiguration. Three of his disciples, Peter, James and John, saw Jesus transfigured, as if he was bathed in white light, talking to two people whom they knew instinctively were Moses and Elijah. The meaning is clear. It is the same as these words of Jesus. Moses represented the Law and Elijah represented the Prophets. The Law and the Prophets are two main parts of the Jewish Scriptures. Jesus did not come to destroy the Old Testament but to fulfil it.

Each paragraph begins 'You have heard ...' and gives an example of a command from the Jewish law. Then Jesus reinterprets it.

Matthew 5:21–26 Murder

According to Jesus it is not enough simply not to murder. The anger which might lead to murder must also be controlled. If there was no hatred there would be no murder. Jesus warns against using insults such as the Aramaic word 'Raca' – traitor. Even calling someone names shows lack of respect. Jesus emphasises this point in verse 22: 'anyone who says, 'You fool!' will be in danger of the fire of hell.'

Jesus warns his audience that religious practices are hypocrisy unless people sort out their differences first before going to worship God. There is no point offering gifts to God otherwise. Nor should there be any delay in making reconciliation. It is as urgent as sorting out legal matters in everyday life before the case against you gets out of control.

Matthew 5:27–30 Adultery

Adultery, having sex with someone else's wife or husband, was a serious matter and the penalties were severe. Guilty women could be stoned to death.

According to Jesus, however, the thoughts that lead to sinful actions must also be controlled:

> *But I tell you that anyone who looks at a woman lustfully has already committed adultery with her in his heart.*
>
> (Matthew 5:28)

The teaching is meant to remind people that we all are tempted to do wrong, however virtuous we think we are.

Nowadays we accept that it is normal for healthy males and females to think about sex and most Christians assume the teaching is against getting obsessed with lustful thoughts. The whole Sermon on the Mount is about the motives behind the actions that people do. Christians believe that sexual behaviour should be motivated by love not by lust.

Gouging out the right eye and cutting off the right hand (v. 29–30) are usually interpreted as metaphors to illustrate how seriously Christians should take the idea of trying to be pure in thought and action.

FOR DISCUSSION

Some Christians say that according to the Sermon on the Mount sinful thoughts are as bad as sinful actions. How far do you think that is what the Sermon teaches?

There is a saying, 'There but for the grace of God go I.' What do you think it means?

Matthew 5:31–32 Divorce

Jesus quotes Deuteronomy 24:1 about divorce. Jewish law allowed men to write a certificate of divorce. Jesus makes marital unfaithfulness the only legitimate justification. Remarriage after divorce is also criticised.

There are different attitudes among Christians towards divorce:

• Some Christian traditions forbid divorce. The Roman Catholic Church, for example, teaches that marriage is a sacrament. This means that marriage is one of the ways in which God's grace is poured out on human beings. Obviously, for Christians who do not believe in divorce, remarriage is out

of the question unless the previous partner has died. Sometimes a marriage can be annulled, as if it had never taken place. This is very rare and applies to situations where, for example, the couple had not consummated the marriage by sexual intercourse.

• Some Christian traditions allow divorce. They quote Mark 10:2–12 where the Pharisees asked Jesus whether it was lawful for a man to divorce his wife. At that time, talking about divorce was a tricky situation. John the Baptist had been put in prison for condemning the marriage of Herod of Galilee to Herodias who had been divorced from Herod's brother. Jesus answered by referring the Pharisees back to the teaching of Moses in Deuteronomy 24:1 (see above). Jesus took the opportunity to explain that Moses allowed divorce because of human failure but it was meant to be the exception not the rule. It is in this passage in Mark that Jesus goes on to say that marriage was instituted by God and 'what God has joined together let man not separate.'

Matthew 5:33–37 Oaths

An oath is a sacred vow. It is a promise made in the name of God. To break such a promise means not only that you have told a lie but also you have taken God's name in vain.

Jesus says here that people should not swear by anything. Swearing to tell the truth implies that you are prepared sometimes to tell a lie.

Many Christians take literally the command not to swear an oath. For the majority this means that they are careful not to use bad language. For others it means also that they will not swear on a Bible in a court of law nor will they swear their acceptance of a creed. The Society of Friends, often called Quakers, is one Christian denomination known for living by this principle.

Truthfulness and honesty are important. The Ten Commandments tell people not to bear false witness; not to tell lies. Christians who apply the principles of the Sermon on the Mount say that you can tell a lie without saying anything. If you miss out some important fact deliberately, in order to deceive somebody, then you have told a lie.

Matthew 5:38–42 An Eye for an Eye

Jesus reminds his audience of the Jewish law of punishment which is found in Exodus 21:24, Leviticus 24:20 and Deuteronomy 19:21. The law of Moses recommended an eye for an eye and a tooth for a tooth. In other words it limited the revenge that could be taken. The punishment should fit the crime. Exact compensation was recommended rather than endless feuds. This law is not unique to Judaism. There are parallels in other ancient laws, e.g. in the code of Hammurabi. This was a very humane law, especially at the time it was written.

The stele of Hammurabi, dated about 1750 BC.

Jesus says that if someone hits you on the right cheek, instead of taking the revenge to which you are entitled, turn the other cheek, your left cheek, to the person who is hitting you. This principle applies to all situations. If someone claims your tunic, give your cloak as well. When the Roman soldier is entitled to ask you to carry his gear for one mile, take it two miles.

This is a challenging passage to anyone who reads it. Do not take revenge, do not retaliate, do not seek retribution. Some readers, not only Christians, take it so literally that they become pacifists. They will not go to war and they will not use force in any situation. Other people see it as an ideal to aim towards.

Matthew 5:43–48 Love Your Enemies

It was logical to go on to talk about loving your neighbour after talking about revenge because the Jewish Law itself says in Leviticus 19: 18 'Do not seek revenge or bear a grudge against one of your people, but love your neighbour as yourself.'

Jesus talked about the importance of the command to love your neighbour in Mark 12:28–34 (see below). It is not one of the Ten Commandments but it summarises some of them.

When Jesus was asked, 'Who is my neighbour?' he told the parable of the Good Samaritan to illustrate that your neighbour means everybody including your enemies (Luke 9:25–37).

The same point is made in the Sermon on the Mount. Jesus takes the command to love your neighbour and extends it to include not only neighbours but enemies as well.

> *But I tell you, love your enemies and pray for those who persecute you.*

This unconditional love for every individual person is meant to reflect God's love and to be the distinctive mark of Christians. The Greek word for such love is 'agape'.

The final verse of this chapter says, 'Be perfect, therefore, as your heavenly Father is perfect.'

- Either it means: By copying the behaviour laid down in the Sermon, by the power of the Holy Spirit, Christians can become more and more like Jesus, the example of perfect humanity.
- Or: The chapter is giving guidelines of an extreme ideal example for Christians to aim towards though it would be unrealistic to think they could ever totally achieve such a standard.

By using this command to be perfect, Jesus was echoing Leviticus 19:2 where the Hebrews are told to

'Be holy because I, the LORD your God, am holy.' People sometimes think the Sermon on the Mount is just ethical teaching about living in a decent society but this verse makes it clear that, like the Mosaic Covenant Law, the ethics of the Sermon on the Mount are based on the character and nature of God.

THINKING POINT

Was Jesus making things easier – or harder?
There are some important points to remember about the teaching of Jesus about the Jewish Law:

- The Jewish leaders stressed the importance of right actions; Jesus extended this to include the intentions and motives.
- The Jewish leaders kept the letter of the law; but Jesus looked also at the spirit of the law and its purpose.
- The commandments tended to be negative in that they emphasised what people should not do. Jesus emphasised positive principles like 'love your neighbour' which could be applied to any situation.

MATTHEW CHAPTER 6

The Sermon on the Mount was probably used to instruct new converts how to live the Christian life. It is still used for this purpose today.

Chapter 5 showed the sort of people Christians should be and the principles by which Jesus said they should live their daily lives.

Chapter 6 moves on to the subject of the teaching of Jesus about religious practices. The chapter starts with three key examples of religious duties:

- giving to the needy
- prayer
- fasting.

The Sermon on the Mount condemns religious hypocrites (the Greek word for play-actors is used here). These are people who pretend to be religious.

Greek actors used to wear masks.

Matthew 6:1–4 Giving to the Needy

The description of the hypocrites broadcasting their good deeds must have made his listeners smile. We get the phrase 'blowing your own trumpet' from these verses. The aim when doing any good deed should be to please God not to impress other people.

The left hand must not know what the right hand is doing. There must be no showing off. True religion is communication between the individual person and God.

Matthew 6:5–8 Prayer

The same points are made concerning prayer. Everything must be done with sincerity. The teaching is not criticising public prayer. It is against making a show of religion and repeating prayers out of habit without thinking about the meaning.

Matthew 6:9–13

Our Father in heaven,
hallowed be your name,
your kingdom come,
your will be done
on earth as it is in heaven.
Give us today our daily bread.
Forgive us our debts,
as we also have forgiven our debtors.
And lead us not into temptation,
but deliver us from the evil one.

Jesus, like many rabbis, gave his disciples a pattern for praying.

The pattern for prayer starts with praise and adoration to God using the title 'Father' which Jesus himself used when praying.

The believers in expressing their hope that God's kingdom will come are volunteering to help bring about God's plans for the world.

Requests for daily necessities follow. Both physical needs such as bread, the basic food, and spiritual necessities such as forgiveness.

Finally there is a petition for protection.

Sometimes a doxology (words of praise) is added: 'For yours is the kingdom, the power and the glory for ever. Amen.' This doxology probably reflects a prayer of King David in 1 Chronicles 29:11.

> *Yours, O Lord, is the greatness and the power*
> *and the glory and the majesty and the splendour,*
> *for everything in heaven and earth is yours.*
> *Yours, O Lord, is the kingdom;*
> *you are exalted as head over all.*

FOR DISCUSSION

Christians believe that this prayer is as appropriate for believers now as it was for those in the early church.

Look at each phrase in the Lord's Prayer and discuss the extent to which this is true.

Matthew 6:14–15 Forgiveness

Sayings about forgiveness continue the theme of sincerity in prayer. The idea is that someone who is genuinely grateful to God for being forgiven will forgive other people.

Matthew 6:16–18 Fasting

Fasting is a sign of repentance. The Pharisees encouraged fasting on Mondays and Thursdays in the daytime. John the Baptist's disciples fasted. Jesus said his disciples would fast when they had good reason to do so.

The early Christians did not seem to take these

THINKING POINTS

If your brother sins rebuke him, and if he repents, forgive him. If he sins against you seven times in a day, and seven times comes back to you and says, 'I repent,' forgive him.' (Luke 17:3–4)

Peter, one of the Apostles, asked Jesus: 'Lord, how many times shall I forgive my brother when he sins against me? Up to seven times?' Jesus answered, 'I tell you, not seven times, but seventy–seven times.' (Matthew 18:21–22)

Do you think Jesus means that there should be no forgiveness on the seventy-eighth time?

What if the person does not repent?

If God knows what you need before you ask him, why do people pray?

verses in the Sermon on the Mount to condemn all fasting. There is evidence that they fasted on Wednesdays and Fridays, as well as during times such as Lent.

The point being made is the same as in the examples of giving charity and praying. It is not fasting but hypocrisy which is being condemned.

Matthew 6:19–24 Treasures in Heaven

This collection of sayings is about having priorities in life. The contrast is made between treasures on earth and treasures in heaven. Worldly treasures do not last. Spiritual wealth lasts forever.

Believers are told to set their heart on things that last; to focus on concerns which bring light into their lives.

Money, property and material possessions should not be allowed to rule a Christian's life. Money should not become a god.

THINKING POINT

How far do you think the themes in these verses echo the same ideas as those in the Beatitudes?

Matthew 6:25–34 Do Not Worry

A person does not have to be rich to show too much concern for worldly possessions. Worrying and being anxious about material things is another sign of getting life out of perspective.

The text says that worrying in advance about what might happen tomorrow is a waste of time and energy.

This does not mean that Christians should not plan sensibly for the future. It is again a matter of priorities. 'Seeking first the kingdom and his righteousness' puts things into perspective.

MATTHEW CHAPTER 7

Matthew 7:1–6 Judging Others

This is a warning about the need to think carefully before criticising others. People making the judgement will have no excuse if they do the same thing because they cannot say that they did not know what should be done and what should not be done.

The saying 'casting pearls of wisdom before swine' comes from this passage. We use it to mean do not waste your breath trying to teach people who are determined not to listen. Both pigs and dogs were unclean to Jews. The actual purpose of including these sayings at this point in the chapter, however, is not clear and Christians have differing suggestions about the meaning. It may be that this was a common saying at the time and the Jewish audience certainly would be familiar with Proverbs where (in 9:7–8 and 23:9) there are warnings about wasting time on discussions with people who are cynical about spiritual matters.

Matthew 7:7–12 Ask, Seek, Knock

These verses continue the theme of prayer. The passage is encouraging Christians to pray confidently, believing that their prayers will be answered and that God knows what is best for them.

Verse 12 is often called the Golden Rule. The story goes that a Gentile asked the Rabbi Hillel to teach him the Jewish Law while the Rabbi was standing on one foot. Hillel answered, 'Whatever is hateful to you, do not do to others.'

In the Sermon on the Mount, Jesus turns the negative saying into the positive form of the command, 'In everything, do to others what you would have them do to you.'

Again Jesus emphasises the continuity with the Jewish Scriptures, 'For this sums up the Law and the Prophets.'

Matthew 7:13–14 The Narrow and Wide Gates

The Sermon on the Mount ends with a series of warnings about the need to make the right choice. It is easy to follow the crowd on the broad road to destruction and hell. The gate to the narrow path is hard to find but it leads to eternal life.

Matthew 7:15–23 A Tree and Its Fruit

The warning against false prophets says that the good and bad prophets can be recognised by their good or bad deeds. At the same time, however, there is the warning that people should make sure that the deeds they do in God's name are according to God's will and not done for the wrong reasons. References to 'that day' in the Bible usually mean the Day of Judgement. Only those obedient to the will of God will enter heaven.

Matthew 7:24–29 The Wise and Foolish Builders

The final warning in the Sermon on the Mount likens the listeners to builders. They can be wise or foolish builders. They have a choice. They can build their house on rock or on sand. They can put the teachings into practice or they can ignore them.

Matthew concludes the Sermon on the Mount by reporting the response of the crowds to the teaching. They were amazed because Jesus taught 'as one who had authority'. Jewish scribes and teachers of the law usually argued from scripture and tradition, quoting the chain of people who had given various interpretations. The repetition of the phrase 'But I tell you' is seen by Christians as evidence of this special Messianic claim to authority.

THE TWO GREAT COMMANDMENTS

One of the teachers of the law came and heard them debating. Noticing that Jesus had given them a good answer, he asked him, 'Of all the commandments, which is the most important?'

'The most important one,' answered Jesus, 'is this: "Hear, O Israel, the Lord our God, the Lord is one. Love the Lord your God with all your heart and with all your soul and with all your mind and with all your strength." The second is this: "Love your neighbour as yourself." There is no commandment greater than these.'

'Well said, teacher,' the man replied. 'You are right in saying that God is one and there is no other but him. To love him with all your heart, with all your understanding and with all your strength, and to love your neighbour as yourself is more important than all burnt offerings and sacrifices.'

When Jesus saw that he had answered wisely, he said to him, 'You are not far from the kingdom of God.' And from then on no one dared ask him any more questions.
(Mark 12:28–34)

The question about the greatest commandment was a common topic for debate. In his answer, Jesus does not choose one of the Ten Commandments but another passage from the books of Moses, Deuteronomy 6:4–5. This is the great Jewish declaration of faith which is called the Shema.

Jesus adds a second command from the books of Moses, 'Love your neighbour as yourself.' It comes from Leviticus 19:18. Loving your neighbour does not mean the person who lives next door, though it includes them. According to Jesus, it means loving every person you encounter.

In John's gospel Jesus says, 'A new command I give you: Love one another.' (John 13:34)

Loving God and loving other people are two positive principles which cover all the Ten Commandments. They also cover inward intentions as well as outward actions.

Jesus did not invent these two principles and he was not disagreeing with the teachings of Judaism. As the lawyer says in his reply to Jesus, the Jewish Scriptures put religious and moral teaching of the Law above ceremonies and sacrifices.

Besides the teaching about the greatest commandment, this gospel incident also shows Christians that the Jewish Scriptures are the foundation and preparation for the teaching of Jesus.

THE ROLE OF MARY AS EXPRESSED IN THE HAIL MARY AND THE CATECHISM

The Hail Mary is one of the most common of prayers used by Roman Catholics.

Hail Mary, full of grace,
The Lord is with thee.
Blessed are thou among women,
And blessed is the fruit of the womb, Jesus.
Holy Mary, Mother of God,
Pray for us sinners, now and at the hour of our death.
Amen

'Dead Christ in the Arms of the Virgin Mary' by Luis de Morales.

The Catechism of the Roman Catholic Church teaches that there were many holy women in the Bible such as Sarah, Rebecca, Rachel, Miriam, Deborah, Hannah, Judith and Esther but Mary was the purest of them all. She obeyed God's wishes without question.

This is seen when she is told that she will be the mother of Jesus and says: 'Behold I am the handmaid of the Lord; let it be [done] to me according to your word.'

Mary's faith never changed even when Jesus was being crucified.

Mary is the supreme model of Christian faith because she believed that 'nothing will be impossible with God', 'For he who is mighty has done great things for me, and holy is his name'.

Sometimes Mary is described as the 'new Eve'. She was preserved from all stain of original sin.

In 431 CE the Council of Ephesus said that Mary truly became the Mother of God by the human conception of the Son of God in her womb.

THE IMMACULATE CONCEPTION

To be the mother of Jesus, Mary was saved from the moment of her conception. That is what the dogma of the Immaculate Conception teaches.

The most Blessed Virgin Mary was, from the first moment of her conception, by a singular grace and privilege of almighty God and by virtue of the merits of Jesus Christ, Saviour of the human race, preserved immune from all stain of original sin.

Mary was blessed more than any other living person and remained free of every personal sin for her whole life.

MARY'S VIRGINITY

The Church teaches that Jesus was conceived solely by the power of the Holy Spirit in the womb of the Virgin Mary.

The Virgin Birth was an act of God which humans cannot be expected to understand: 'Behold, a virgin shall conceive and bear a son.' (Isaiah)

The Church teaches that Mary remained a virgin throughout her life and that James and Joseph, 'brothers of Jesus', are the sons of another Mary, a disciple of Christ, whom Matthew calls 'the other Mary'.

THE ASSUMPTION

When the time came for her life on earth to end, Mary, who had remained free from all sin, fell asleep (Dormition) and was taken up body and soul into heaven.

'Annunciation' by Robert Campin c.1410–1440.

ICT FOR RESEARCH

Look up Mary (Virgin Mary) in Encarta to help you consider the importance of the role of Mary for Roman Catholics.

PRACTICE EXAMINATION QUESTIONS

1 (a) **What do Christians believe about the Trinity?** (*8 marks*)

You are being asked to show that you know that the Trinity is central to Christian monotheistic belief and that Christians believe that the one God is the three persons, Father, Son and Holy Spirit in unity. You may wish to develop your answer by quoting a Creed or by adding some of the beliefs about the three persons in your own words. Any accurate information about Christian beliefs about the Trinity is acceptable.

(b) **Explain how beliefs about the afterlife might affect the way Christians live.** (*7 marks*)

A brief account of the beliefs about the afterlife is needed but the focus of the question is your explanation of the ways in which these beliefs might affect the lifestyles and outlooks of Christians in the modern world. Remember that Christians do not believe in reincarnation. They believe they only have this one lifetime. Try to think of positive effects not only negative fears of judgement. After all, the message is said to be 'good news'.

(c) **'It is impossible to follow the example of Jesus, so there is no point in trying.'**
Do you agree? Give reasons to support your answer and show that you have thought about different points of view. (*5 marks*)

You may agree or disagree but remember to include arguments in support of your opinion and to consider the reasons why other people might disagree with your view. You may wish to discuss certain parts of the quotation in particular. For example you may think that it is difficult but not impossible or you may think that no one can be like Jesus but there is every point in trying. Look back at the teachings you have included earlier in the question and see if they might be relevant to the argument.

2 (a) **What beliefs about Jesus are stated in a Creed you have studied?** (*8 marks*)

Either quote the Creed, selecting the relevant parts, or give the general sense of the beliefs about Jesus contained in the Creed you have studied.

(b) **Explain the importance for Christians of the two great commandments (Mark 12:28–34).** (*7 marks*)

You will need to make it clear what the two great commandments are but the focus of the question is an explanation of their importance as two general positive principles from the Jewish Scriptures given by Jesus, which may be said to sum up the Ten Commandments and which may provide guidelines for Christians when trying to solve ethical dilemmas.

(c) **'How you behave is more important than what you believe.'**
Do you agree? Give reasons to support your answer and show that you have thought about different points of view. You must refer to Christianity in your answer. (*5 marks*)

You have already written about the behaviour expected of Christians and about their beliefs. Which do you think is the more important and why? Consider other opinions. For centuries Christians have debated the relationship of faith and good deeds and how far salvation depends on believing in Jesus rather than on following his teachings and example. Look up James 2:14–17 before you reach any final conclusions.

3 (a) **In the Sermon on the Mount which people did Jesus say were blessed (happy)?** (*8 marks*)

You are expected to show your knowledge of the Beatitudes (Matthew 5:1–12) where the teachings of the Sermon on the Mount are introduced by a section on true values for living and real happiness. You may quote the passage or paraphrase it. The Sermon on the Mount is a set text. Do not attempt a question like this unless you have some knowledge of the general content of the text.

(b) Explain how the teaching of Jesus about judging other people might affect the lives of Christians. (7 marks)

Sometimes questions simply ask you to explain teachings. You would select the teachings and show your understanding of the meaning of the verses. This question is encouraging you to give examples of Christian behaviour to show that you understand. It is also giving you the opportunity to point out that teachings are not interpreted the same way by all Christians. Relevant verses might include the comment after the Lord's Prayer about forgiving others and the beginning of Matthew 7 about not judging others. You may wish to use other parts of the Sermon on the Mount about anger or revenge or about love for enemies. You may widen the explanation to include other teachings of Jesus about forgiveness which are not in the sermon.

(c) 'The Sermon on the Mount is not meant to be taken literally, especially about turning the other cheek.'

Do you agree? Give reasons to support your answer and show that you have thought about different points of view. (5 marks)

When you plan the final part of a question, it is wise to look back at what you have written for the earlier parts because those answers may suggest points which you can develop in the discussion. In this question you are likely to find yourself discussing whether the Sermon is meant to be an ideal to aim towards or a practical application of Christian principles possible with the power of the Holy Spirit.

4 (a) Describe what Jesus taught about prayer in the Sermon on the Mount. (8 marks)

You are expected to show some knowledge of the contents of the Sermon. You may quote or paraphrase the teaching. The Sermon not only contains the Lord's Prayer, as a pattern for prayer, and encouragement to pray confidently but also warnings against reciting prayers automatically without any thought of the meaning and against doing religious practices to look good in front of other people.

(b) Explain why Christians should not worry nor be anxious, according to the teaching in the Sermon on the Mount. (7 marks)

Some credit will be given for demonstrating knowledge of the passage where Christians are told not to worry in Matthew 6:25–34 but good answers are likely to be those which try to explore some of the possible meanings and implications of the teaching.

(c) 'Christians need to plan for the future; they cannot just live for today.'

Do you agree? Give reasons to support your answer and show that you have thought about different points of view. (5 marks)

Though Christians are like everybody else in that they have to try to balance different parts of their lives, the fact that this question so far has been about the Sermon on the Mount should indicate to you that the best discussions are likely to refer back to the text. The Sermon on the Mount is about priorities and the Christian perspective for living. Look back to earlier parts of the question to see why the teachings on prayer and not worrying might lead some Christians to think they should or should not plan for the future.

2

FESTIVALS, FASTS AND SPECIAL DAYS

Most religions have days and times of year that are special or sacred.

Having a regular cycle of events to plan, look forward to and experience together strengthens community spirit and the celebrations remind believers of past events in their religion and the beliefs they have in common.

The major Christian festivals are based around the life of Jesus and they have been celebrated since at least the fourth century CE. The most important early Church calendar was compiled by Furius Dionysius Philocalus about 354 CE.

Advent marks the beginning of the Christian year. It falls on the Sunday nearest to 30 November.

In the Christian calendar many festivals do not fall on the same date each year. The Christian year includes some fixed dates, such as 25 December on which the birth of Jesus is celebrated. There are also other festivals that are movable feasts because their dates change each year depending on the date of Easter.

Some Christians celebrate more festivals, fasts and special days than others. Some celebrate none at all. The Roman Catholic and Orthodox churches observe many festivals and holy days including Saints' days. The Lutheran churches and Anglican churches celebrate the seasons of the Christian year in much the same way and at the same time as Roman Catholic churches. The Society of Friends tends to be at the other extreme. Friends, often called Quakers, do not celebrate any festivals because, to them, all times and all days are special. Most Protestant Christians, however, celebrate the major festivals, particularly those that have a scriptural origin.

There are three great festivals celebrated annually throughout the Christian world. They are:

- Christmas, which remembers the birth of Jesus
- Easter, which celebrates the death and resurrection of Jesus
- Pentecost (Whitsun), when the disciples were given the Holy Spirit.

Each of these festivals has a time of preparation leading up to it.

THINKING POINT

In the western world when do we start the New Year?

When does the school year begin?

When does the financial year begin?

Do you know of any other New Year celebrations?

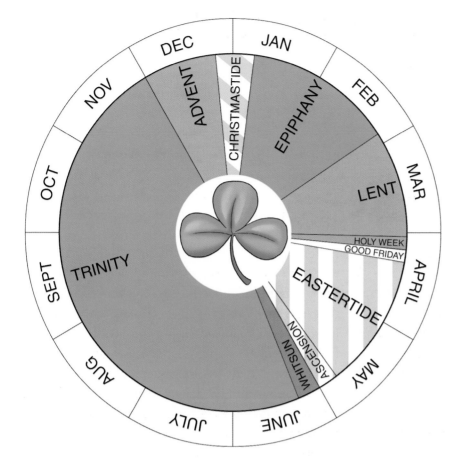

Diagram of the Christian year. The colours are those of the cloths used to cover the altar and the lectern in church. The vestments, the special clothes worn by the priests at church services, are in the same colours.

The Julian calendar is still the official calendar of many eastern Orthodox churches whilst the Christian year in the West is based on the Gregorian calendar so holy days celebrated by both the eastern and western churches do not always fall on the same date (see note on calendars).

What season is it in the church in the photograph?

THE JULIAN AND GREGORIAN CALENDARS

Throughout history, scholars have had problems measuring time.

Today, scientists measure the length of a day to be 23 hours 56 minutes and 4.1 seconds. For convenience, days are divided into 24 hours.

Some people measure time by a lunar calendar based on the phases of the moon. Their day begins at sunset. The new moon marks the start of the new month. The length of time from one new moon to the next new moon is 29½ days. There are 354 days in a lunar year. The lunar year is shorter by ten or eleven days than the solar year (measured by the sun). Muslims still use a lunar calendar.

When Christianity began, the calendar in common use was a solar calendar that had been authorised by Julius Caesar about 50 years before the birth of Jesus. It is known as the Julian calendar. Solar calendars are based on the sun and have 12 months of differing lengths to make it easier to fit annual events to the same season each year. Each day starts at midnight.

The Julian calendar had been designed by astronomers and was considered to be very reliable. It had leap years to help keep the system in line but in fact it was 11 minutes 14 seconds too long each year. Those few minutes added up to one whole day every 128 years. By 1582 the Julian calendar was ten days out of step with the solar year.

Pope Gregory XIII ordered a revision of the calendar. It was necessary, first, to jump ten days. To make sure that future years would stay accurate, it was decided to make an adjustment to leap years. Only one in every four years ending in 00 were to be leap years. For example, 2000 was a leap year but 2100, 2200 and 2300 will be common years.

The reformed calendar was called the Gregorian calendar. Some non-Catholic countries did not wish to use a calendar authorised by a Pope, even though it was more accurate. For example, Britain and the American colonies did not use it until 1752, Soviet Russia adopted it only after the Russian revolution in 1918 and Greece in 1923.

In Britain the Gregorian calendar was called the New Style calendar to make it more acceptable. By then 11 days needed to be dropped so 3 September became 14 September 1752. There were riots in the streets about the changed calendar and people protested 'Give us back our eleven days!'

LENT

Easter is the most important Christian festival of the year. The season of preparation for Easter is called Lent. It is a time of fasting and spiritual preparation that lasts for 40 days. It starts on Ash Wednesday and finishes at midnight on Holy Saturday, the day before Easter Sunday.

The word 'Lent' comes from an old English word for springtime and the lengthening of daylight which happens in spring.

HOW CHRISTIANS OBSERVE LENT

During Lent Christians remember that Jesus spent 40 days and 40 nights without food in the desert whilst he was preparing for his ministry.

In the Eastern Orthodox churches Lent is actually the eight weeks before Easter. It is longer than 40 days. This is because Saturdays and Sundays are not counted. They are festival days and Jesus said that his followers would not fast at times of rejoicing (Mark 2:18–22).

In the west, only Sunday is treated as a festival so, when the 40 days are counted, only the Sundays are left out.

Lenten Monday is the start of fasting for the Orthodox Christians. In the western churches, the first day of Lent is Ash Wednesday. The name comes from the custom practised by some Christians of rubbing ashes on their foreheads as a mark of sorrow and repentance for the sins committed during the past year. The ashes have been blessed by a priest or a bishop. Crosses in churches are covered with a purple veil to symbolise penitence.

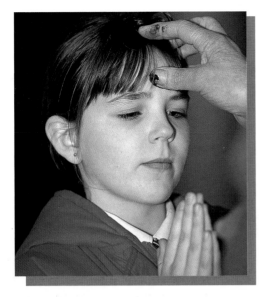

Roman Catholics and some Anglicans use ashes made from the palm leaves used the previous year on Palm Sunday. The priest says, 'Remember that you are dust and unto dust you shall return' to remind Christians that life is short and every day should be taken seriously.

Latin words 'carnem levare' which mean 'to take away meat'. The festivities are full of feasting, merrymaking, music, dancing, masquerades and parades. It is seen as the last opportunity for self-indulgence before the time of self-denial.

ICT FOR RESEARCH

In Encarta, see the photo of Mardi Gras in New Orleans, Louisiana, USA.

The day before Lent is Shrove Tuesday. 'Shriven' means to have your head shaved and some Christians used to shave their heads as part of their penitence at the start of Lent. They would confess their sins to the priest who would declare absolution and impose a penance. Penance is some task that the priest sets the person. The word 'Shrove' has come to mean 'being forgiven'.

It is traditional to eat pancakes on Shrove Tuesday. This comes from the practice of using up all the butter, fat, eggs, milk and cream before the time of self-denial, so these foods would not be wasted. In Britain many villages still celebrate Pancake Day with pancake tossing, races and fancy dress.

In French-speaking countries the pre-Lenten Tuesday is called Mardi Gras (Fat Tuesday). The idea of a carnival leading up to the Tuesday festivities started in medieval Europe and spread to other parts of the world. The word carnival comes from the

In the past, Lent was a very strict fast and involved total abstinence from meats and fats but, through the centuries, the restrictions have been relaxed. Since 1966 only Ash Wednesday and Good Friday are obligatory fasting days for Roman Catholics during Lent. Fasting is not permitted on the Sundays of Lent.

Lent is still a serious and solemn time but nowadays it is more customary for Christians to keep Lent by denying themselves something they enjoy or by trying to live more simply without luxuries.

Lent is seen as an opportunity not only to give up things but to do positive extra activities. The money saved on sweets and luxuries and the time saved by giving up trivial pleasures can be used for helping others. Some Christians give up some of their meals or have a very simple meal together and donate the money they save to charities.

Many Christians learn over the years to look forward to this annual opportunity to take life more seriously and to grow more devout in their faith and practice.

Many churches have Lent Courses of weekly meetings.

FOR DISCUSSION

Have you ever tried to fast or gone without food for some reason? Maybe it was a religious occasion or a sponsored event. Perhaps you had been to see the dentist or you were going into hospital for an operation or you were simply trying to slim. What were your feelings about the experience? How long did the whole thing last? What was the hardest part? What did you miss the most?

Most Christians believe that religious practices should be done for good reasons or they are worth nothing. Do you agree? Suggest reasons for fasting that may not be good reasons.

Some Christians think Mardi Gras festivities contradict the whole spirit of Lent. What do you think?

Lent is the spiritual preparation for Easter. The last week of Lent is Holy Week (see below) and there are special church services which help Christians to meditate on the significance of the events in the last week of the life of Jesus.

Fasting is a great test of self-control. Obviously there is no point in trying to cheat. Christians believe that God sees every action and knows the intention of the heart.

THE SIGNIFICANCE OF LENT FOR CHRISTIANS

Many religions practise fasting. For some religious people, the denial of bodily appetites is part of a strict attitude to life. For others, the discipline is meant to help them to appreciate the things they have.

IN YOUR NOTES OR FOR DISCUSSION

So what reasons are there for fasting?

Start with self-restraint or self-control and make a list of reasons why Christians might decide to observe Lent.

Not only will believers learn to appreciate the good things which they enjoy when they are not fasting but they will learn to distinguish between luxuries and necessities. This will teach them compassion and will result in them being less greedy, less selfish and more charitable towards the needy.

It is not possible to predict all the effects that the observance of Lent might have on people who take part. Sometimes Christians may feel disheartened because they gave in to temptation. The experience might prove, however, to be very positive, not only in the short-term but with long-lasting effects. Struggling against temptation and sharing the experience with other church members can lead to spiritual growth for the individual and the community.

For Christians one main reason for observing Lent is to remember the 40 days Jesus spent in the wilderness. Jesus was preparing for his ministry, facing temptations and resolving to do God's will even though it would lead to his death. Christians remember all this and they take stock of their own lives. They consider the failings of the past year and they resolve with God's help to make a fresh start.

Read the story of the temptations of Jesus in Matthew 4:1–11 or Luke 4:1–13.

The First Temptation of Christ, 1223 AD, from Troyes Cathedral.

Jesus had just been baptised by John the Baptist and he was about to start his ministry. There were three types of temptations which he faced:

- It was very tempting to provide food not only for himself but for the starving poor under the Roman occupation.
- He could have used his power to prove his identity as the Messiah, to himself as well as to everyone else.
- He could have used the wrong means to gain followers and establish a political kingdom.

Jesus rejected all of these temptations.

HOLY WEEK AND EASTER

HOLY WEEK

Holy Week is the last week of Lent. It starts with Palm Sunday and ends on the Saturday at midnight. During Holy Week, Christians remember the last week in the life of Jesus.

The events of the last week in the life of Jesus can be pieced together from the gospel accounts.

Diary of the last week in the life of Jesus:

Sunday	Thursday
Palm Sunday – Jesus enters Jerusalem	Maundy Thursday – the Last Supper; the arrest in the garden of Gethsemane
Monday	
Fig Monday – Jesus cleanses the Temple	**Friday**
	Good Friday – trials and crucifixion
Tuesday	
Holy Tuesday – questions from the Jewish leaders	**Saturday**
	Holy Saturday – the body of Jesus is in the tomb
Wednesday	
Spy Wednesday – Judas Iscariot betrays Jesus by arranging his capture	

EASTER

Though Easter Sunday marks the Resurrection of Jesus, for many Christians the Easter festival is considered to last for 90 days. It starts with Lent and lasts until Whitsuntide, 50 days after Easter Sunday.

The word 'Easter' probably comes from the name of Eostre, the Saxon goddess associated with the coming of spring.

For Christians, however, Easter is a religious celebration based on their beliefs about Jesus Christ, in particular the belief that he rose from the dead.

Christians celebrate the resurrection of Jesus Christ on Easter Sunday. It is appropriate that the celebrations are in spring because new life is one of the themes of the Christian festival of Easter.

Christian Easter owes its date, however, to its link with the Jewish Passover. Jesus died during Passover week. The Last Supper was probably a Passover meal. In fact another name for the Christian festival of Easter is 'Pasch'.

'Why is this night different from all other nights?' Passover is a Jewish festival, celebrated in Spring, when Jews remember that they were slaves in Egypt. They eat special food, including lamb and unleavened bread, and drink red wine. The youngest male asks four questions and the answers tell the story of how God led the Jews out of Egypt into their own land.

Because it is connected to the Jewish celebration of Passover Easter can occur as early as March 22 or as late as April 25.

The first Christians differed among themselves on how to calculate the date for Easter Day. They agreed that Jesus died during Passover week so some, particularly Jewish Christians, wanted Easter to be celebrated on 14 Nisan as an extension of the Jewish Passover. The 14 Nisan can fall on any day of the week. The resurrection took place on a Sunday so some other Christians felt that Easter should always

be on a Sunday. The Council of Nicaea in 325 CE ruled that Easter should be on the first Sunday after the first full moon on or after the vernal (spring) equinox.

HOW CHRISTIANS OBSERVE HOLY WEEK AND EASTER

Holy Week begins with Palm Sunday which celebrates the triumphant entry of Jesus into Jerusalem, riding on a donkey. He was greeted by crowds waving palm branches and laying down palm leaves in front of him. Many churches are decorated with palm leaves and each member of the congregation at Palm Sunday services receives a cross made from a palm leaf. In the Eastern Orthodox church, Palm Sunday is known as Willow Day because branches of willow are waved instead of palms.

Sometimes Christians, led by someone carrying a cross, have processions through the streets or round the church.

On Holy Thursday, the Thursday of Holy Week, Christians remember the Last Supper. The day is known as Maundy Thursday. This name comes from the Latin 'mandatum' meaning commandment because of the command which Jesus gave at the Last Supper:

> *A new command I give you: Love one another. As I have loved you, so you must love one another.*
>
> (John 13:34)

Jesus said these words at the last meal which he had with his friends. It took place in the upper room in the house of John Mark's mother in Jerusalem.

There were 13 at the table; Jesus and his 12 apostles including Judas Iscariot. During the meal, Jesus told his friends that one of them would betray him and all of them would desert him. Peter, in particular, insisted that he would never deny his master but Jesus told him that he would do so three times that very night before dawn.

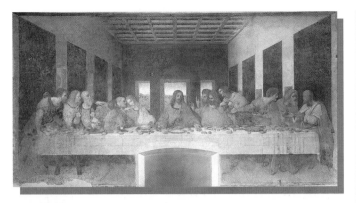

This fresco was painted by Leonardo da Vinci from 1495 to 1497.

ICT FOR RESEARCH

The Last Supper has been a popular theme with artists past and present. Look up other paintings of the Last Supper, for example in Encarta and in the Encyclopaedia Britannica.

The Last Supper was probably a Passover meal.

While they were eating, Jesus took bread, gave thanks and broke it, and gave it to his disciples, saying, 'Take it; this is my body.' Then he took the cup, gave thanks and offered it to them, and they all drank from it. 'This is my blood of the covenant, which is poured out for many,' he said to them.   (Mark 14:22–24)

This Last Supper is remembered and repeated by Christians in a celebration service called the Eucharist, Mass, Holy Communion, the Lord's Supper or the Breaking of Bread. Many churches have a special celebration of this meal on Maundy Thursday to mark the anniversary of the first time Jesus told his disciples to do this.

Often, the service of the Eucharist on this day includes a foot-washing ceremony. The priest or minister washes the feet of some of the congregation. The Pope washes the feet of 12 males.

This is following the example of Jesus who washed the feet of his disciples in the upper room on that last night. Usually a servant would have done this task.

In Britain the king or queen used to perform a foot-washing ceremony. The last time it was done was by James II. The tradition grew that on Maundy Thursday the British monarch would give Maundy money to the poor. Nowadays, specially minted coins are given at a service in a cathedral as an honour to some local elderly Christians. The number of purses given out depends on the monarch's age and the coins are copies of ones used at the time of King Charles I.

After the meal, Jesus went to the Garden of Gethsemane, on the Mount of Olives, to pray. It was there that Judas led the men who would arrest Jesus. The rest of the disciples were waiting for Jesus but they had fallen asleep. In the dark, Judas identified Jesus by greeting his master with a kiss.

Some Christians hold a vigil on the Thursday night. They try to stay awake and pray as they remember the events of that night.

The trial of Jesus before the High Priest took place before dawn and, in the early hours of the morning, there was the trial before the whole Sanhedrin, the Jewish council. Peter had followed the soldiers at a distance into the High Priest's courtyard. There, he lost his courage and three times denied that he knew Jesus.

Good Friday recalls the ordeal of Jesus as he was dragged from place to place, mocked and beaten. The Jewish leaders accused him of blasphemy but the Roman Governor, Pontius Pilate, thought that religious matters were none of his concern. When he realised Jesus came from Galilee, he sent him to be tried by the ruler of Galilee, Herod Antipas, who was in Jerusalem for the Passover. When Herod could not force Jesus to do any miracles, he sent Jesus back to Pontius Pilate.

The Jewish leaders changed the accusation to treason on the grounds that Jesus claimed to be the Messiah, the King of the Jews. Pilate tried to wash his hands of the affair but, when he heard the crowd shouting and the chief priests said 'We have no King but Caesar' Pilate felt pressured into sentencing Jesus to death. The Roman method of capital punishment was crucifixion.

Jesus was crucified on a hill, Calvary, which was known also as Golgotha, the place of the skull. It was the usual place for Roman crucifixions. Two criminals were executed at the same time as Jesus, one on either side of him.

Pilgrims in Jerusalem visit 14 places which are associated with events in the journey of Jesus to the cross. From medieval times, Roman Catholic churches have featured 14 pictures representing these stopping places. They are called the Stations of the Cross and they enable the congregation to make a token pilgrimage. The priest processes round the church and stops at each of 14 pictures where he leads the congregation in meditation and prayer.

Good Friday commemorates the death of Jesus. In most churches Good Friday is a day of fasting, abstinence and penance. Jesus was crucified at the third hour – 9 a.m. Vigils and quiet services are held in many churches throughout the day, especially between noon and 3 p.m. This was the time, according to the gospels, when darkness fell over the land as Jesus was dying.

Christians carrying a cross to Walsingham in Norfolk, on Good Friday.

In some churches the cross or a crucifix is venerated and believers may kiss the feet of the carved figure of Christ on the cross to show their respect and devotion.

In some Orthodox churches, the priest carries an icon (a holy painting) of the body of Jesus or a cloth like a burial shroud. The congregation stand round it as if they were at a funeral. All decorations are taken from Orthodox, Roman Catholic and Anglican churches to make the churches as plain as possible or else black and purple cloths are used to symbolise sorrow and death.

The full story of the last week in the life of Jesus is found in the New Testament gospels:

Matthew chapters 21–27
Mark chapters 11–15
Luke chapters 19–23
John chapters 12–19

Some services are based on the words spoken by Jesus from the cross:

Luke 23:34
Luke 23:43
John 19:26f
Mark 15:34 (quoting Ps 22:1)
John 19:28
John 19:30
Luke 23:46

FOR DISCUSSION

Why, do you think, do Christians give the name 'Good Friday' to the anniversary of the death of Jesus?

Holy Saturday is the last day of Holy Week and was once known as the 'Great Sabbath'. The body of Jesus lay during this day in the tomb which Joseph of Arimathea had given for the burial. The Sabbath is the Jewish day of rest so it was not until the day after the Sabbath that the women came to the tomb of Jesus with spices to anoint the body.

The tomb must have looked very like this one in Jerusalem. In fact, some Protestant Christians say it is the actual tomb in which the body lay.

On the Saturday, Christians get ready for the next day by cleaning the church and preparing fresh altar cloths and vessels. Lent is nearly at an end. Some Christians keep a quiet vigil through the night till dawn.

Easter Sunday is the most joyful day of the Christian year.

Around the world, Christians celebrate the Resurrection in different ways.

Many churches have displays of Easter gardens which are models of the rock tomb showing the stone rolled away from the entrance. They may have been made by the children in Sunday School.

In many churches, a large candle is lit which burns throughout all the services of the Easter festival. It is called the Paschal candle and is a symbol of the presence of the risen Christ, the victory of light over darkness and of life over death. One of the titles Christians use for Jesus Christ is 'The Light of the World'.

Some Easter celebrations are very dramatic. Many Orthodox churches have a service on Saturday night that lasts until Sunday morning. Just before midnight, the whole congregation goes outside leaving the church in darkness and as quiet as a tomb.

The crowd waits outside. There is a shout of triumph which is repeated three times: 'Christ is risen from the dead. By death he has trampled down death. And to those who are in the grave he has given life.' The church doors are flung open like the stone rolled away from the tomb. The priest announces, 'Christ is risen!' The people reply, 'He is risen indeed!' Every person has a candle and the light grows as each candle is lit and then lights another, just like the message of the Resurrection spread from person to person. The people run into the church and the building is flooded with light. Bells are rung and there may be fireworks, bonfires and parties with all the sweet foods which were banned during Lent.

The celebration of Easter continues for another 40 days. The fortieth day is Ascension Day which commemorates the last time the disciples saw the resurrected Jesus. On Ascension Day the Paschal candle is put out.

At Oberammergau in Bavaria a Passion play is performed every ten years. The fortieth performance was in 2000. The tradition began with a vow made by villagers who survived the plague of 1633. They promised to perform a passion play every ten years.

THE SIGNIFICANCE OF HOLY WEEK AND EASTER FOR CHRISTIANS

The events of Holy Week are often called 'The Passion'.

Easter is considered to be the most important feast in the church year because it celebrates the resurrection of Jesus Christ after the crucifixion.

From the start of Holy Week, Christians remember not only what happened but think also about the meaning of the events. The whole passion story explores Christian beliefs about the identity of Jesus.

On Palm Sunday, the crowd shouted, 'Hosanna. Blessed is he who comes in the name of the Lord,' which was the regular greeting for pilgrims entering Jerusalem. The gospel writers saw this as being very appropriate for the Messiah entering the holy city. By the end of the week, they were shouting, 'Crucify him'.

When Jesus entered the city on Palm Sunday, some of the crowd were shouting out about 'the Son of David' entering 'David's city'. The crowds wanted to be freed from Roman rule. They were expecting an earthly political kingdom and a triumphant warrior king like King David who made Jerusalem the capital of his kingdom.

Christians see the event as Jesus fulfilling a prophecy in Zechariah 9:9:

> *Rejoice greatly, O Daughter of Zion!*
> *Shout, Daughter of Jerusalem!*
> *See, your king comes to you,*
> *righteous and having salvation,*
> *gentle and riding on a donkey,*
> *on a colt, the foal of a donkey.*

During the rest of Holy Week, Christians continue to reflect on the nature and work of the Messiah, the Christ, and on the true meaning of 'the kingdom of God'.

On Maundy Thursday Christians may think about the significance of the fact that Jesus washed the feet of the disciples.

> *When he had finished washing their feet, he put on his clothes and returned to his place. 'Do you understand what I have done for you?' he asked them. 'You call me "Teacher"' and "Lord", and rightly so, for that is what I am. Now that I, your Lord and Teacher, have washed your feet, you also should wash one another's feet. I have set you an example that you should do as I have done for you.'*
> (John 13:12–15)

This act was an example of humility and of service and love for others. One of the titles which Jesus used of himself in the gospels was 'the Servant' which comes from a prophecy in Isaiah 53 about a suffering servant. Jesus combined this idea with another Messianic title in Mark 10:45.

> *For even the Son of Man did not come to be served, but to serve, and to give*
> *his life as a ransom for many.*

The name Eucharist comes from the Greek word for thanksgiving. When Christians think about the Last Supper, they feel gratitude and joy. They are sad because Jesus died but they believe that his death made it possible for the sins of the whole world to be forgiven. They also feel grateful because of a promise that Jesus made.

At the Last Supper Jesus said, 'I tell you, I will not drink of this fruit of the vine from now on until that day when I drink it anew with you in my Father's kingdom.' (Matthew 26:29)

When Christians read this saying, it reminds them that sharing the Eucharist is a foretaste of the Messianic meal which they believe Jesus promised all believers would share.

> *People will come from east and west and north and south, and will take their*
> *places at the feast in the kingdom of God.*　　　　　　　　　(Luke 13:29)

In the events of the Thursday night there are some powerful moments in the narrative, not only at the Last Supper but also later in the Garden of Gethsemane.

> *Going a little farther, he fell with his face to the ground and prayed, 'My*
> *Father, if it is possible, may this cup be taken from me. Yet not as I will, but*
> *as you will.'*　　　　　　　　　　　　　　　　　　　　　(Matthew 26:39)

> *Then he returned to his disciples and found them sleeping. 'Could you men*
> *not keep watch with me for one hour?' he asked Peter. 'Watch and pray so*
> *that you will not fall into temptation. The spirit is willing, but the body is*
> *weak.'*　　　　　　　　　　　　　　　　　　　　　　(Matthew 26:40–41)

Christians share the suffering of Jesus and gain insight into the meaning of his death. Many will identify with his followers in their grief and guilt for betraying and denying Jesus. Then they will pray in humility and gratitude, believing that, because of the death of Jesus, their sins and failings can be forgiven.

FOR DISCUSSION

What do you think the painter is trying to express about the crucifixion?

'The Agony in the Garden of Gethsemane' by El Greco.

'Christ of St. John of the Cross' by Salvador Dali.

A still taken from the film 'Jesus of Nazareth'.

A well-known Christian hymn explains what Christians believe about the meaning of the death of Jesus:

There is a green hill far away,
Without (outside) a city wall,
Where the dear Lord was crucified
Who died to save us all.

We may not know, we cannot tell,
What pains he had to bear;
But we believe it was for us
He hung and suffered there.

He died that we might be forgiven,
He died to make us good,
That we might go at last to heaven,
Saved by his precious blood.

There was no other good enough
To pay the price of sin;
He only could unlock the gate
Of heaven, and let us in.

O dearly, dearly has he loved,
And we must love him too,
And trust in his redeeming blood,
And try his works to do.

People have always celebrated the coming of Spring. Easter eggs go back to ancient spring festivities long before Christianity just like Easter bunnies and other fertility symbols. Even hot cross buns, at one time in England only eaten on Good Friday, probably began as a pagan symbol of the phases of the moon. Some Christians use secular symbols and give them a Christian meaning. To them, eggs contain new life and that is the joyful theme of Easter.

The Resurrection appears in the New Testament gospels:

Matthew chapter 28
Mark chapter 16
Luke chapter 24
John chapters 20–21

The belief in the resurrection of Jesus has always been at the heart of the Christian message. It confirmed in the minds of his followers that Jesus was the Messiah. It proved that good will triumph over evil. It also gave them hope that death is not the end. The Christian belief in life after death is based on the victory of Jesus over death.

In I Corinthians 15, Paul says that Christ is the firstfruits, the guarantee that believers also will conquer death.

FOR DISCUSSION

Do you think Christians should campaign against the commercialisation of Easter?

Pope John Paul II called Christians 'an Easter People'. What do you think he meant?

Easter Monday has become a time for protest marches such as anti-nuclear demonstrations. Sometimes Christians of different denominations join together on these walks. Do you think this is an appropriate way for Christians to observe Easter?

ADVENT, CHRISTMAS AND EPIPHANY

Advent marks the start of the cycle of events which makes up the Christian year.

Advent is four weeks of prayerful preparation before Christmas.

The date of Christmas Day is always 25 December. This day was kept by the Romans as Midwinter Day. Christians took over the date to celebrate the birth of Christ.

On the twelfth day of Christmas the festivities come to an end with the feast of Epiphany.

The accounts of the events surrounding the birth of Jesus are found only in the gospels of Matthew and Luke.

It is clear that all four gospel writers and other New Testament writers share the same beliefs about Jesus even though they do not tell the actual story of his birth.

HOW CHRISTIANS OBSERVE ADVENT, CHRISTMAS AND EPIPHANY

ADVENT

The word 'advent' means 'coming'. The Bible readings for Christian services during the four weeks of advent refer not only to the coming of the baby Jesus at the first Christmas but also to the coming of Christ at the end of history. Christians prepare spiritually for the coming of Jesus.

Near Christmas, carol services take place. Many people feel that it is bad luck to sing carols at any time of year other than at the Christmas season.

In Anglican churches there is a popular carol service with nine lessons from the Bible showing how God created humans, cares for them and sent his Son to be born in Bethlehem. The readings include prophecies about the Messiah.

In 1918 King's College Cambridge began its festival of lessons and carols. This has continued to the present day and is seen on television by millions of people.

KING'S COLLEGE CHAPEL

A FESTIVAL OF NINE LESSONS AND CAROLS

CHRISTMAS EVE
2002

Bishop Gilbert of Truro started the festival of nine lessons and carols in Victorian times.

Nativity plays about the birth of Jesus are performed in churches.

Manger scenes are set up in the church portraying the birth of Jesus in the stable.

Some churches have a Christingle service during Advent. This custom comes from Scandinavia. Each child receives an orange and a candle.

The red ribbon is the blood of Jesus and the love of God embracing the world.

Advent is a time of hope, prayer and preparation. Christians may use Advent calendars and Advent candles to remind themselves that the Christmas festival is coming nearer. Advent wreaths of evergreens have four red candles to mark off the four weeks. Holly, ivy, mistletoe and other evergreens have been used in winter to decorate homes in Europe for centuries.

In Britain, in Victorian times, Christmas puddings were made before the start of

The candle represents Jesus, the light of the world.

Advent. Stir-up Sunday was the last Sunday before Advent and all people in the household would have a stir of the pudding using a wooden spoon. Stirring the pudding was meant to bring good luck. There are various customs associated with advent and many of them go back to pre-Christian times when the mid-winter solstice was approaching. Making a pudding of the dried fruits which had been stored to last through winter was part of cheering up the people. Winter was half over. The sun was returning.

CHRISTMAS

The word 'Christmas' comes from Christ's mass, the service held in church to celebrate the birth of Jesus. Nobody knows the exact date on which Jesus was born. In fact, nobody knows the exact year in which Jesus was born. From 354 CE when Pope Gregory introduced the date, Christians have held services on 25 December to celebrate the birth of Jesus.

Many Christians go to midnight services and receive holy communion on Christmas Eve in candle-lit churches. There are family services on the morning of Christmas Day too.

Christmas is family time. Children receive presents, supposedly brought by Santa Claus (Saint Nicholas). Gifts and cards are exchanged by adults too. Special foods are eaten such as turkey, mince pies and Christmas pudding. Decorations, trees with trimmings, lights, holly and mistletoe are hung in houses and outside. Nowadays Christmas trees and evergreen plants are found in churches though, for a long time, they were usually not placed in Christian places of worship because of their pagan associations.

For some Christians, Christmas is the time they make a special effort to help other people. They visit hospitals and old people's homes. They may spend Christmas Day helping to provide a meal and party for the elderly, the lonely and the homeless.

Some of the Christmas traditions date back to mid-winter pagan festivities, Yuletide in Europe and the Roman festival of Saturnalia.

There was a time in England when the celebration of Christmas was forbidden. It was in 1647 after the civil war when Oliver Cromwell and the roundheads were in power. The Puritans disliked the pagan origins of many Christmas traditions and they distrusted dancing, drama and any activities which they considered to be frivolous pastimes. Even the singing of Christmas carols was banned. Carols were not sung in the towns any more but many traditions were kept alive in the countryside.

The later Protestant non-conformist Christian denominations which started in England were not so puritanical about music. The Methodists in particular made a great contribution to the singing of hymns and carols. One of the founders of Methodism, Charles Wesley (1707–78) wrote 'Hark the Herald Angels Sing' (see Chapter 8).

It was during the reign of Queen Victoria (1819–1901) that the popularity of carol singing and celebrating Christmas was fully restored. Two Victorian scholars, William Sandys and Davies Gilbert, travelled round the countryside collecting the old Christmas music.

Many customs now associated with Christmas were introduced in Victorian Britain. Having Christmas trees is said to have been started by Prince Albert, Queen Victoria's husband, who brought the idea from Germany. The sending of Christmas cards began and Charles Dickens (1812–70) wrote the novel *A Christmas Carol* in which the heart of Scrooge was softened when the crippled boy, Tiny Tim, said, 'God bless us all.'

The Salvation Army are a familiar sight in the streets around Christmas.

Some Christians do not celebrate Christmas. Some believe that all days are special and so they do not celebrate any feast days or festivals. Some do not celebrate Christmas because they know that Jesus was not born on 25 December and they see the festivities as a pagan tradition. Some Christians are reluctant to encourage the greed and worship of money that exploit Christmas and are contrary to the values which Jesus taught. Some Christians keep the religious traditions but try to avoid the commercialisation. Other Christians welcome all the glitter and sparkle of the festival, hoping that it might remind some people in a busy secular world about the birth of Jesus and the Christian message.

ICT FOR RESEARCH

In Encarta: see Christian festivities in Guatemala where Mayan and Christian traditions are combined.

FOR DISCUSSION

How do you think Christians should celebrate Christmas?

Christianity tends to absorb earlier customs rather than to try to get rid of hem. How far do you think this is a good idea?

EPIPHANY

Epiphany comes from the Greek word for 'displaying' or 'revealing'. Three stories are read from the New Testament during this festival in western churches:

- Matthew 2:1–12 – the showing of the baby Jesus to the Magi (wise men) who travelled from the east, following a star which they believed would lead them to a new king. The idea that there were three Magi comes from the three gifts they brought: gold, frankincense and myrrh. In the Eastern churches, Orthodox Christians have a tradition that there were 12 wise men and the Bible story is part of the Christmas services. Often the wise men are portrayed as following the star to the stable. The story in Matthew implies that Mary was in a house and the baby Jesus was nearly two years of age.
- John 2:1–11 – the first miracle which was the turning of water into wine by Jesus at a wedding in Cana.
- Matthew 3:13–17 – the baptism of Jesus in the River Jordan by John the Baptist when a voice from heaven identified Jesus as God's son.

The night before Epiphany is called Twelfth Night and it is the time when Christmas decorations are taken down. Epiphany itself is sometimes called Twelfth Day and in the western calendar it takes place on 6 January. In England, the sovereign offers gold, frankincense and myrrh at the altar in the Chapel Royal at St. James' Palace in London.

THE SIGNIFICANCE OF ADVENT, CHRISTMAS AND EPIPHANY FOR CHRISTIANS

Advent, Christmas and Epiphany are all joyful celebrations but they have a serious side too. Even during advent when preparing for the celebrations of the birth of Jesus, Christians are also thinking about death, judgement, heaven and hell. They study the Jewish Scriptures which Christians call the Old Testament. These books show how God revealed himself throughout history (see Chapter 7). They also contain prophecies about the Messiah which Christians believe were fulfilled in Jesus.

- Christmas celebrates the birth of Jesus.
- The humble birth in the stable reminds Christians that the gospel message is for everyone. This includes the weak, the poor, the homeless and the outcasts.
- Ordinary people, like the shepherds, and rich people, like the wise men, are all welcome and equal when kneeling before the baby.
- The angels sing about peace on earth. Christmas cards often contain paintings of angels and symbols of peace, such as the dove.
- The role of motherhood is important in the story.
- The holy family is a reminder of the importance of families and children.
- At Christmas, Christians remember that God's greatest gift is Jesus himself who is their saviour and friend.
- Candles remind Christians that Jesus is the Light of the World.

Most of these themes can be understood easily. Believing in Jesus, caring for other people, giving to charities and praying for peace on earth are all part of the effects of taking the message of Christmas seriously. There are some other aspects of the Christmas story which are important in understanding the significance of this festival for Christians:

- The gospel stories of the birth of Jesus are full of references to the fulfilment of prophecy and show the beliefs that Christians have about Jesus being the Messiah.
- Christians believe that the birth of Jesus was part of God's plan for the salvation of the world.
- Christian teaching refers to the birth of Jesus as the Incarnation. The word Incarnation means embodiment in flesh. This is the belief that God in the person of Jesus became human.
- The gospel of John tries to express what Christians believe about this:

In the beginning was the Word, and the Word was with God, and the Word was God. . . .The Word became flesh and made his dwelling among us. We have seen his glory, the glory of the One and Only, who came from the Father, full of grace and truth. (John 1:1, 14)

Epiphany means making known who Jesus really was. In particular, Epiphany refers to the revelation to the Gentiles of Jesus as the Saviour. This is seen by Christians as part of a great master plan by which God will bring about the salvation of the world and it is the main significance of the visit of the wise men. Traditionally in the West the magi were named as Balthazar, king of Arabia, Melchior, king of Persia, and Casper, king of India.

The symbolism of the gifts is said to be gold for kingship, frankincense for priesthood and myrrh for suffering and death. These are a reminder to Christians that Christmas was only the start of the story.

PENTECOST (WHITSUN)

Pentecost (Whitsun) is seven weeks after Easter Sunday. The festival marks the gift of the Holy Spirit of Christ to his followers after his resurrection and ascension.

Most of the followers of Jesus were Jews. They were in Jerusalem for the Jewish Feast of Shavuot, Pentecost, which takes place 50 days after Passover. The name 'Pentecost' comes from the Greek for fiftieth day. The Jewish festival mainly celebrates the giving of the Law to Moses on Mount Sinai. There were 120 of the followers of Jesus in the upper room where they had gathered behind locked doors. The story of what happened can be found in Acts 2.

HOW CHRISTIANS OBSERVE PENTECOST (WHITSUN)

This festival used to be a favourite time for baptism ceremonies of new converts. Those being baptised were dressed in white so it became known as White Sunday or Whitsun.

In some areas of Britain there are Whit walks where Christians join in a procession round the local streets as a witness to the community of their Christian faith.

In church on Whit Sunday Christians read about the dramatic coming of the Holy Spirit. There was a sound like a stormy wind and what seemed to be flames of fire settling on the heads of the believers. They all began 'speaking in tongues' and soon were communicating the gospel to the people in Jerusalem.

Some Christians see this account of the power of the Holy Spirit as picture language whilst others accept it as a literal happening.

The religious phenomenon of making ecstatic utterances is called glossolalia (from the Greek for speaking in tongues). It is listed in the New Testament as one of the spiritual gifts of the Holy Spirit (I Corinthians 12 to 14).

The New Testament account of the happenings on the Day of Pentecost includes Peter's sermon to the crowd. The sermon is a summary of the beliefs of the first Christians and reading it at Whitsun reminds Christians of the roots of their faith.

Christianity is a missionary religion. Jesus told his followers to spread the message and promised to send the Holy Spirit to help them. Prayers and sermons on Whit Sunday emphasise the need for Christians to spread the gospel and show the fruit of the spirit in their lives:

The fruit of the Spirit is love, joy, peace, patience, kindness, goodness, faithfulness, gentleness and self-control.
(Galatians 5:22–23a)

THE SIGNIFICANCE OF PENTECOST (WHITSUN) FOR CHRISTIANS

Pentecost celebrates the coming of the Holy Spirit. It is often said to be the birthday of the church because it was the start of the mission to preach the gospel to all people. Luke says in Acts 2 that there were 3000 converts by the end of the day of Pentecost.

At the Ascension Jesus made this promise to his followers:

> *But you will receive power when the Holy Spirit comes on you; and you will be my witnesses in Jerusalem, and in all Judea and Samaria, and to the ends of the earth.*
>
> (Acts 1:8)

Instead of being afraid and hiding behind locked doors, the first Christians, full of the Holy Spirit, boldly witnessed to other people. Christians use the word 'witnessing' to refer to preaching the gospel.

The message that they were spreading is found in the sermon that Peter preached to the crowds on the day of Pentecost.

> *God has raised this Jesus to life, and we are all witnesses of the fact.*   (Acts 2:32)

At first the crowd thought that the disciples were drunk. Peter pointed out that it was only nine in the morning. He said the coming of the Holy Spirit had been prophesied in the Jewish Scriptures and quoted the prophet Joel.

> *In the last days, God says, I will pour out my Spirit on all people.*   (Acts 2:17)

Christians believe that the Holy Spirit continues to work in the world. The power of the Holy Spirit, they believe, is what inspires people and gives special charismatic gifts, such as the ability to preach, teach, heal, prophesy and speak in tongues like the disciples did at Pentecost. Most important of all, the Holy Spirit helps them to spread love in the world (see Chapter 1 on beliefs about the Holy Spirit).

THINKING POINT

Why was the Jewish Feast of Pentecost an appropriate time for the Holy Spirit to be given to the followers of Jesus?

SUNDAY

Sunday gets its name because the Greeks and Romans named the day in honour of the Sun god. It is the first day of the week.

Christians call Sunday the Lord's Day (as in Revelation 1:10). For Christians it is the weekly remembrance of the Resurrection of Jesus on the first day of the week. It is also the day of rest for most Christians.

HOW CHRISTIANS OBSERVE SUNDAY

Justin Martyr (c. 100–165 CE) wrote 'And on the day which is called the day of the sun there is an assembly . . .' and he described how Christians read from the gospels or from the Old Testament, had a sermon, prayed and celebrated the Lord's Supper.

Many Sunday services follow this pattern to the present day though some follow the order of service in a prayer book or missal whilst others have more informal meetings. Music plays an important part in some services. Sermons may be longer in some denominations (see Chapter 5).

Many Christian children attend Sunday Schools. Robert Raikes (1736–1811), a newspaper publisher in Gloucester, was interested in prison reform. He thought there would be fewer young offenders if children had some Christian teaching. In 1780 he managed to get the support of a local Anglican vicar. The teachers were lay people who held the classes in their own homes at first. The progress of the experiment was reported in the newspaper and the idea caught on. Most churches of all denominations nowadays have Sunday schools.

Sunday is recognised by most Christians as a day of rest and recreation but different branches of the Christian church observe Sunday in different ways. In countries which are mainly Roman Catholic, religious services take place on Saturday night and Sunday morning but the remainder of the day is given to sport and leisure activities. Strict Protestant churches, however, keep Sunday more like a Jewish Sabbath on which no work is allowed nor frivolous activities. There are many Christians who are somewhere between these two approaches to the observance of Sunday.

In theory the Society of Friends has no holy days because all days are holy but meetings for worship are held on Sundays.

Some Christians, such as the Seventh Day Adventists, believe that the weekly holy day should be Saturday. This is because the fourth of the Ten Commandments refers to the seventh day, the Sabbath day, which should be kept holy.

THE SIGNIFICANCE OF SUNDAY FOR CHRISTIANS

Most of the first Christians were Jews and at first Christianity was seen as a Jewish sect. They were followers of 'the Way'. They were Messianic Jews. At first they continued to observe Jewish customs. They were used to worshipping on the Jewish Sabbath, the seventh day. The Sabbath lasted from Friday sunset to Saturday sunset. Jesus used to attend synagogue on the Sabbath. Paul on his missionary journeys always tried to preach in the synagogue first in places he visited. Increasingly, however, Christians found that they were rejected by Jewish communities.

It seems that from the beginning, Christians had their own meetings together for the breaking of bread on the first day of the week, the day of the Resurrection, Sunday. (Acts 20:7 mentions such a meeting where Paul was preaching. 1 Corinthians 16:2 also assumes this was the practice.)

The meetings were in people's houses (1 Corinthians 16:19, Colossians 4:15).

As more and more Gentiles flocked to join Christianity, the links with Judaism weakened. Eventually the fact that a person worshipped on a Sunday rather than a Saturday became a means of identifying Christians at the time when Christianity was illegal in the Roman Empire. Persecution stopped when the Emperor Constantine became a Christian. In 321 CE, to encourage people to worship in church, he decreed that all work should cease on Sunday except necessary farming.

The idea of resting for one day in seven is a very ancient custom. It was one of the laws in the Code of the Babylonian king Hammurabi in the eighteenth century BCE.

Sabbath means resting day and one of the Ten Commandments is about keeping one day for rest and worship.

> *And God blessed the seventh day and made it holy, because on it he rested from all the work of creating that he had done.* (Genesis 2:3)

> *Remember the Sabbath day by keeping it holy. Six days you shall labour and do all your work, but the seventh day is a Sabbath to the Lord your God. On it you shall not do any work, neither you, nor your son or daughter, nor your manservant or maidservant, nor your animals, nor the alien within your gates. For in six days the Lord made the heavens and the earth, the sea, and all that is in them, but he rested on the seventh day.* (Exodus 20:8–11)

The commandment also gives a religious reason for observing the Sabbath. It is a weekly celebration of the completion of creation. The Genesis account of creation says that God rested on the seventh day.

The New Testament gospels give many examples of arguments between Jesus and the Jewish religious authorities about law-keeping. Jesus told his followers in the Sermon on the Mount that they should keep the law. Christians still keep the Ten Commandments. They try to follow the example of Jesus in the way they do this.

The Jewish religious authorities said Jesus broke the Sabbath when he healed people. Jesus said:

> *. . . it is lawful to do good on the Sabbath.* (Matthew 12:12b)

He also said:

> *The Sabbath was made for man, not man for the Sabbath.* (Mark 2:27b)

John's gospel contains an account of Jesus healing a cripple and telling him to take up his bed and walk. The man is accused by the authorities of breaking the Sabbath by carrying the mat which was his bed. John writes:

> Jesus said to them, 'My Father is always at his work to this very day, and I, too, am working.'
>
> (John 5:17)

The story about the Sabbath shows that the arguments between Jesus and the Jewish leaders were caused by his claim to have authority from God and his challenge to their negative ways of keeping the law. The words of Jesus in the story point to an important belief about the Sabbath – that the holy day is the most appropriate day for doing good positive things.

At the time of the Reformation, Scottish and English Protestant reformers especially John Knox (1514–72) were strict Sabbatarians. This means they took the fourth commandment very literally. They accepted that Sunday was the Christian day of rest but they treated it like a Jewish Sabbath.

The Lord's Day Observance Society was formed in 1831. Proposals to run railway trains on Sundays was a big controversy at the time. Nowadays, increased leisure and technology have led to the relaxing of laws about weekend activities.

Most Christians feel that it is their duty to worship on Sunday and try to attend their place of worship. They could stay at home to worship God but they feel that the discipline of going to church is useful. The sermons may encourage people to put their beliefs into action and working together helps build community spirit.

> Let us not give up meeting together, as some are in the habit of doing, but let us encourage one another – and all the more as you see the Day approaching.
>
> (Hebrews 10:25)

Jesus said:

> For where two or three come together in my name, there am I with them.
>
> (Matthew 18:20)

FOR DISCUSSION

What are the best ways that Christians might keep Sunday as a holy day?

Are rest and recreation more important now than they were in the past?

How might going to church on Sunday affect a person during the rest of the week?

THE ASSUMPTION OF THE BLESSED VIRGIN

The Assumption of the Blessed Virgin Mary (the Feast of Dormition in the Orthodox Church) takes place in mid August.

This is a very holy occasion, particularly in the Greek Orthodox church. There is a vigil in the evening and the lighting of the Holy Fire at midnight. Usually, there is a barbecue and whole lambs are roasted on a spit. Community sports are a feature of the celebrations. Football and hunting are popular activities at this time.

To Orthodox, Roman Catholic and many Anglican Christians Mary is the first among saints. The Orthodox Christians describe Mary as:

- Theotokos – Mother of God
- Aeiparthenos – Ever Virgin
- Panagia – Fully holy.

Assumption means reception or being accepted. The Assumption of the Virgin Mary into heaven means that Mary fell asleep (Dormition) and was the first of redeemed humanity to be received by Jesus in heaven.

Mary is believed to have been conceived immaculately which means 'without sin'. All her life she was a virgin and devoted her life to her son, Jesus. Because Mary was without sin she could not die as other people do and so at the end of her life, when she fell asleep, she was assumed into heaven. Roman Catholics say that Mary was then crowned Queen of Heaven by Jesus. The assumption was first celebrated in the sixth century as Dormition and was made an article of faith (something which Catholics must believe) by Pope Pius XII in 1950. It is celebrated in the Roman Catholic Church on August 15.

PRACTICE EXAMINATION QUESTIONS

1 (a) **Describe how Christians keep Lent. (*8 marks*)**

You may wish to concentrate on describing how one particular Christian denomination keeps Lent, when preparing for Easter, but try to include some positive spiritual preparations besides describing what people give up when they are fasting. Technically Lent goes from Ash Wednesday to Easter Saturday so you will need to keep the descriptions brief, especially of Holy Week. The explanations why Christians keep Lent in this way belong in the next part of the question. That is why it is wise to read all parts of the question and plan what you are going to write before you start.

(b) **Explain how keeping Lent might affect the life of a Christian. (*7 marks*)**

When answering questions which invite you to explain the relevance and application of religious practices, try to think of positive effects as well as negative drawbacks and long-term not simply short-term results.

(c) **'Religious fasts are for adults, not for children.' (*5 marks*)**

Do you agree? Give reasons to support your answer and show that you have thought about different points of view. You must refer to Christianity in your answer.

Finally you are being asked to think back over what you have written. You may write about fasting in general but you need to refer to Christianity and Lent is very relevant. How far might what you have written apply to a child? What age of child? Suggest reasons why children may benefit from fasting and reasons why they should not do so. Lent is a preparation for Easter. Is there a suitable compromise which could be made?

2 (a) **Describe a Sunday service in a Christian place of worship. (*8 marks*)**

You may choose any Christian place of worship but it would be sensible to name the denomination of the service you are describing. Try to give as much detail of the service as possible.

(b) **Explain why Christians celebrate Pentecost (Whitsun). (*7 marks*)**

A good explanation is likely to include some reference to the account of the coming of the Holy Spirit at Pentecost in Acts 2. The fact that it is seen as the birthday of the church is important and that it celebrates the on-going work of the Holy Spirit.

(c) **'Regular weekly services are more significant for Christians than annual festivals.' (*5 marks*) Do you agree? Give reasons to support your answer and show that you have thought about different points of view.**

Finally you are being asked to discuss whether weekly services such as the one you described are more significant than an annual celebration such as Pentecost. Remember that the context is Christianity. Suggest arguments for each point of view. It may be that in the end you argue that both are significant.

3 (a) **Describe the religious ways Christians celebrate Christmas. (*8 marks*)**

There are many ways that Christians celebrate Christmas so try to select those which could be described as religious. Going to church services is an obvious way but there are many practical helpful activities in which Christians get involved that may equally be described as 'religious'. If you are uncertain about some of the items you wish to include, you may take the opportunity to explain their relevance in the next part of the answer.

(b) **Explain the meaning of Christmas for Christians.** (*7 marks*)

Your answer might include reference to the birth of Jesus and the ideas which may be drawn from the Gospel stories about the message being for the poor as well as the rich, the hope of peace on earth and showing love. The key ideas to explain are Christian beliefs about the Incarnation and the fulfilment of prophecies about the Messiah.

(c) **'All Christian festivals are of equal importance.'**

Do you agree? Give reasons to support your answer and show that you have thought about different points of view. (*5 marks*)

Any festivals may be used but Christmas is an obvious festival to include in this argument. You have already explained its meaning so you can refer back to your explanation. Easter is said to be the most important festival and you could justify this argument. You are free, however, to suggest that it depends on the context. A case might be made in favour of the statement depending on what sort of importance is meant.

4 (a) **Describe how Christians in Holy Week remember the death of Jesus.** (*8 marks*)

You may concentrate on one denomination or you may give a general description across denominations but notice that the question does not ask for an account of everything in Holy Week. You are

being asked to be selective. Good Friday will be a focus of the answer but brief reference may be made to other parts of the week if they are related to remembering the death of Jesus.

(b) **Explain how and why celebrating Easter might affect a Christian's life.** (*7 marks*)

You are being given the opportunity to explain the meaning, significance and importance of Easter and how it might affect the life of Christians. You may deal with 'how' and 'why' separately or together. Easter is meant to be a time of rejoicing and of hope though, of course, the effects might be different for individual Christians. Some effects may be short-term, others long-term or cumulative in that every year the faith of the believers grows stronger.

(c) **'Christians should not buy Easter eggs and Easter cards.'**

Do you agree? Give reasons to support your answer and show that you have thought about different points of view. (*5 marks*)

Commercialisation of Christmas is often criticised by Christians and many of the same points apply to the way people make money at Easter. The celebrations at both times of year replaced ancient pagan seasonal rites and this might be another reason for some Christians to feel uncomfortable. You are free to argue in favour of any point of view but remember to give reasons for your opinions and to consider how other people might answer your arguments.

3

MAJOR DIVISIONS AND INTERPRETATIONS

ROMAN CATHOLIC, ORTHODOX AND PROTESTANT CHRISTIANS

The Christian message soon spread through the Roman Empire and beyond.

Over the centuries, the Christian Church split into different denominations. The denominations can be grouped into three main branches:

- The Roman Catholic Church – more than half of the world's Christians
- The Orthodox Church – less than ten per cent
- The Protestant Church – approximately one-third

Only about five per cent of Christians in the world do not belong to one of these three branches.

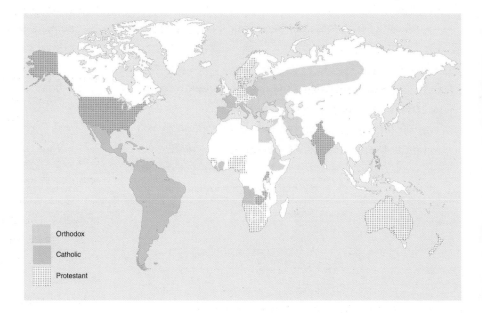

Statistics vary but one thing is clear: In 1900 most of the world's Christians lived in Europe. This is no longer the case. Here are year 2000 statistics:

South America	583.5 million
Europe	420.8 million
Africa	392.8 million
North America	269.3 million
Asia	224.5 million
Former USSR	29 million

One-third of the world is nominally Christian.

THE ROMAN CATHOLIC CHURCH

The word 'Church' means the whole body of believers when it is being used to translate the Greek word 'ekklesia'. This is the word used in the New Testament for the community of Christians. It means an assembly of people.

The word 'Catholic' from the Greek word Katholikos means universal.

The word 'Roman' is used because the city of Rome in Italy is the centre and headquarters of the Roman Catholic Church.

Jerusalem was the place where the followers of 'The Way' started the movement that would become the Christian Church. Rome, the capital city of the Roman Empire, came into the history of the Church almost immediately. According to the Acts of the Apostles in the New Testament, when Simon Peter preached in Jerusalem at Pentecost, the crowd included:

> ... visitors from Rome (both Jews and converts to Judaism) ... (Acts 2:10b–11a)

The book of Acts goes on to tell how the Apostles spread the message from Jerusalem. A large part of Acts tells about the missionary journeys of Paul. At the end of the book, Paul is a prisoner awaiting trial in Rome.

All roads led to Rome and all roads led from Rome so when the gospel reached the capital city it was the guarantee to the Christians that the promise of Jesus would be fulfilled and the message would reach the ends of the earth.

> But you will receive power when the Holy Spirit comes on you; and you will be my witnesses in Jerusalem, and in all Judea and Samaria, and to the ends of the earth. (Acts 1:8)

The Christian Church also spread through different groups of society. Again, this is shown in the Acts of the Apostles. The circle grew wider and wider:

- from Palestinian Hebrew-speaking strict Jews
- through Hellenistic Greek-speaking liberal Jews
- to proselytes who were full converts to Judaism,
- as well as to God-fearing Gentiles (non-Jews)
- and totally pagan Gentiles.

It was part of Paul's theology that God's plan for the world included spreading the gospel to the Gentiles.

By the time Paul reached Rome, there was already a group of Christians in the city.

Christian theologians say that God chose the perfect time of history for the spread of the gospel of Jesus Christ. There were three significant factors which existed at the time:

- The Jewish religion – its monotheistic beliefs and moral code were attractive ideas to Gentiles who were tired of the religious practices used in the worship of the Greek and Roman pantheons of gods and goddesses. Judaism was not a missionary religion, though proselytes were accepted. Christianity, on the other hand, actively sought converts. The Diaspora (Greek for Dispersion) of the Jews through the Mediterranean lands in previous centuries meant that there were Jews in many places in the Roman Empire. Synagogues were places where Christian missionaries could start preaching. If there was no synagogue or Christians were banned from it, they could on most occasions still use Jewish ideas as a familiar basis on which to build the message for anyone who would listen.
- The Greek Language – the koine (common Greek) had been spoken from the fourth century BCE around

the Mediterranean regions and in the Middle East. In the past, the Greeks had ruled most of the areas which became part of the Roman Empire. The Greeks believed in education and encouraged the use of Greek. The Roman language was Latin but it took a long time for it to be established as the main language of the Roman Empire. The letters which were sent to the churches and which became part of the New Testament were written in Greek.

- The Roman Empire – The Pax Romana (the peace of Rome) enabled Roman citizens to cross boundaries between countries and travel around the empire on the Roman roads.

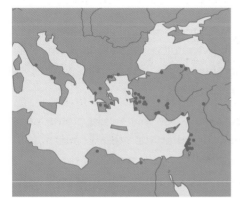

Number of Christian churches in 100 CE   *Number of Christian churches in 200* CE   *Number of Christian churches in 300* C

Antioch in Syria was the place from where Paul set out on his missionary journeys. Paul and Barnabas reported back there that God had 'opened the door of faith to the Gentiles'. The followers of the Way were first called by the nickname 'Christians' at Antioch.

Jerusalem was obviously of great significance, also, because that was where the Christian Church began. At first, James, the brother of Jesus, led the Jerusalem Christians. When, in Acts 12, Peter escaped from prison he reported to James.

The tomb of St. James in Jerusalem.

James presided over the Council of Jerusalem in 49 CE when the Christian leaders were discussing the implications of accepting Gentiles as Christians. Acts 15 tells the story of this council.

There were two important issues about the mission to the Gentiles:

- Could non-Jews become Christians?
  The Church in Jerusalem had already decided that Gentiles could become Christians. This decision was based on Simon Peter's report about the conversion of the Gentile centurion Cornelius and the falling of the Holy Spirit on his Gentile household. The whole story can be found in Acts 10 and 11. Simon Peter reminded the Council of this incident.

- Did the Gentiles have to become Jews first?
  This second issue was the main subject of debate at the Council. If the Gentiles had to become Jews first it would mean that the males would have to be circumcised. It would also mean that everyone would have to keep not only the Ten Commandments but all the rest of the Jewish laws and rules as well. There are 613 mitzvot (rules) which are found in the Torah.

In the past, according to Paul when he was writing to the church in Galatia, even Peter had been influenced by strict Jewish Christians and had stopped eating with Gentiles.

At the Council of Jerusalem, Simon Peter spoke out clearly on this matter of principle:

> *Now then, why do you try to test God by putting on the necks of the disciples a yoke that neither we nor our fathers have been able to bear? No! We believe it is through the grace of our Lord Jesus that we are saved, just as they are.*
>
> (Galatians 15: 9–11)

James summed up at the end of the council:

> *It is my judgment, therefore, that we should not make it difficult for the Gentiles who are turning to God. Instead we should write to them, telling them to abstain from food polluted by idols, from sexual immorality, from the meat of strangled animals and from blood.*
>
> (Galatians 15:19–20)

Gentiles were expected to keep the essential morality of the Ten Commandments and to avoid food associated with sacrifice to idols.

There is no doubt that Christianity would not have spread so easily among the Gentiles if they had been required to become Jews first. The decision of the Council, however, was one of the reasons Christianity moved further from its roots in Judaism.

There was a Jewish Revolt in 66 CE against the Romans. The whole war did not stop until the fall of Masada to the Romans after a siege in 72–73 CE but the most significant event of the war was the fall of Jerusalem and the destruction of the Temple in 70 CE. This seems to have been one of the practical reasons why the church in Jerusalem stopped being the centre for Christianity. There continued to be Christians in Jerusalem but the city of Rome eventually became the centre of the Church.

Significant places in early Church history.

Peter and Paul were martyred during the reign of Nero when the Christians were being persecuted after a fire broke out in Rome. According to tradition, Peter asked to be crucified upside down. He did not feel worthy to be crucified in the same way as his master.

Whether Peter was called the Bishop of Rome is uncertain but to Christians in Rome, he was their leader because Jesus had appointed him to look after the Church. Since that time, according to Christians, the touch of Jesus has been passed on through Peter and his successors when they lay their hands on others.

The New Testament shows the apostles appointing bishops and deacons. The word 'bishop' comes from the Greek word 'episkopos' meaning overseer, someone who looks after things. At first, a bishop looked after one church but gradually became in charge of a larger area (see the Pope in Chapter 5).

In the second and third centuries the bishops became more and more important. Historians disagree about how soon the Bishop of Rome became the most important bishop rather than 'primus inter pares', Latin for 'first among equals'. The Bishops of Rome, Antioch, Jerusalem and Alexandria had more authority than other bishops.

The Roman Empire had grown too big. It had been divided into two halves by Emperor Diocletian (284–305 CE) with a co-emperor in charge of each half to make it easier to rule. Constantine became Emperor of the whole Roman Empire in 312 CE. He made the city of Byzantium into his new capital and renamed it Constantinople. Nowadays it is called Istanbul. The city was further east than Rome and seemed more central for ruling the extended empire. In fact, the West became weaker and Rome was attacked by Alaric the Goth in 410 CE. Constantinople grew in importance. Christianity in the two cities developed differently but the Church remained united.

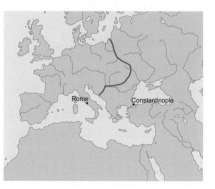

In 440 CE Leo I reminded everybody that his authority could be traced all the way back to Peter who was the first Bishop of Rome, or Pope. The word Pope comes from the Greek 'pappas' meaning 'father'. The Council of Chalcedon in 451 CE agreed with his claim to be the head of the Church and confirmed that 'both God and Peter have spoken through Leo'.

The Christians remained united under the Pope in Rome until a disagreement about doctrine caused a split between the eastern and the western parts of the Church. This division is known as the Great Schism of 1054.

THE FIRST ROMAN EMPEROR TO BECOME A CHRISTIAN

There were rivals of Constantine who wanted to be Emperor. He defeated his last opponent, Maxentius, at the battle of Milvian Bridge in Italy in 312 CE. According to one tradition Constantine's mother Helena was a Christian. He prayed to her god for help before the battle.

And while he was thus praying with fervent entreaty a most incredible sign appeared to him from heaven . . . a cross of light in the heavens, above the sun, and an inscription 'Conquer by this' attached to it.

Eusebius, Bishop, church historian, friend of Constantine

Constantine fought under the sign of the cross and won. Though Constantine was converted to Christianity he continued to worship Sol Invicta, the Sun God and kept the image of the sun on his coins as well as the Chi-Rho Christian symbol. Before his death he was baptised. Constantine was the first Roman Emperor to become a Christian.

Constantine made Christianity a tolerated religion (Latin: religio licita). He did not make it the state religion but his patronage meant that it was fashionable to be a Christian. Before long,

Christianity was the religion of the Roman Empire. There was a rise in monasticism in Christianity soon afterwards which historians suggest resulted from Christianity becoming more popular. For some Christians it was an attempt to return to the purity of Christianity in the past.

FOR DISCUSSION

Suggest reasons why some people might think that having a state religion is a good idea and some people might not.

Consider the different reasons why religious people might become monks and nuns.

THE ROMAN CATHOLIC AND ORTHODOX SPLIT

The Roman Catholic Church is the oldest branch of Christianity.

The word Orthodox comes from the Greek 'orthos' meaning 'correct' or 'straight' and 'doxa' meaning 'belief' or 'opinion'.

The split in 1054 is sometimes also called the East–West Schism.

The argument is usually said to be about the 'filioque' phrase in the Nicene Creed.

'Filioque' means 'and from the Son'. It affirms that the Holy Spirit not only comes from God but also from the Son. It was an attempt to get rid of a heresy, Arianism. Arius in Alexandria had taught that Christ was more than mere human but not fully God. The filioque debate started in Spain and Germany but gradually the idea was accepted in Rome. The eastern part of the Church thought there should have been a council to decide any alterations to the creed. At the time they accepted the Pope of Rome was the first among equals but they did not think that he could make new laws. They were also concerned that the additional idea might compromise the teaching about the Trinity because the Holy Spirit was being placed a little further away from God the Father.

Envoys were sent from Pope Leo IX in Rome to Constantinople. When the debaters could not agree, the representatives from Rome placed a document on the altar saying that the clergy of Constantinople were no longer in union with Rome. The Patriarch of Constantinople, Michael Cerularius, equally condemned the West. In short, they excommunicated each other.

After the split, the two parts of the church, the east and the west, continued developing in their own distinctive ways. Historians think that the crusades from the eleventh to the thirteenth centuries had a large part to play in confirming the East–West split in Christianity. The Christian knights from Europe were supposed to be helping Christians in the East to keep the pilgrimage routes open and to oppose the spread of Muslim control of the Holy Land. When knights from the West pillaged and looted Constantinople in 1204, the split between East and West was definite. The Byzantine Empire grew weaker and eventually became part of the Ottoman Muslim Empire. The division in Christianity between East and West continued until December 1965 when the two traditions began official attempts to discuss their differences.

THE DIFFERENCES BETWEEN ROMAN CATHOLICS AND ORTHODOX CHRISTIANS

AUTHORITY AND ORGANISATION

The Roman Catholic Church is based in Italy where the leader, the Pope, lives in the Vatican. The Vatican is a city-state within the larger city of Rome, the capital of Italy. The Roman Catholic Church is the largest religious organisation on earth. It has a hierarchy of authority with the Pope at the top (see Chapter 5).

Apart from not accepting the authority of the Pope, the organisation of the Orthodox Church is similar to that of the Roman Catholic. Church leaders in the East are called patriarchs not bishops and the areas they supervise are called patriarchates in which there are dioceses.

Unlike the Roman Catholic tradition, the Orthodox Church accepts married men as priests though in both Churches single men who become ordained must remain unmarried. Orthodox priests are bearded and dress differently.

The patriarch of Constantinople continues to be seen as more senior than the patriarchs of Alexandria, Antioch and Jerusalem but he does not rule over them.

The Orthodox Church continues to make decisions by councils as it did in the past. Orthodox Christians live in many countries including the United Kingdom but mainly the Orthodox Church is a collection of national self-governing Churches. The best known are probably the Greek Orthodox Church and the Russian Orthodox Church but there are many more, some continuing from ancient times, like the Coptic Church in Africa and the Armenian Church.

Over the centuries, the various branches of the Orthodox Church have developed differently. For example, in 1917 during the First World War, there was much reorganisation among the Balkan churches and the Serbian Orthodox Church grew in importance. The collapse of the communist governments in the East at the end of last century has led to further changes in the situations of many branches of the Orthodox Church.

ICT FOR RESEARCH

Look up the Orthodox Church in Australia to see how many different branches of Orthodoxy are represented there.

BELIEFS

The beliefs of Roman Catholics and Orthodox Christians are very similar.

Christians in both traditions believe in the Trinity, redemption through Jesus Christ and transformation in their lives by the power of the Holy Spirit. Both also show respect to the Virgin Mary. Orthodox Christians refer to Mary as Theotokos, which is Greek for 'God bearer'. This is a reference to Mary in her role as mother of God (see Chapter 8).

WORSHIP

The Roman Catholic Church and the Orthodox Church use different calendars for the church year. Both celebrate Christmas and Easter as the two major festivals but the celebrations are not always held on the same date.

Easter celebrations of the Resurrection are often very dramatic in the Orthodox churches (see Chapter 2).

Nowadays, since the second Vatican Council (1962–65), Roman Catholic church services are in the language of the local people but for centuries they were in Latin, the language of the Romans.

Services in Orthodox churches are led by the priest. There are no seats because the congregation stands for the service, sometimes bowing and kneeling. A choir may lead the singing but there are no musical instruments (see Chapter 8). Many Orthodox churches use the vernacular, the national language, for their services and have done so since the first Christian missionaries arrived in their country. In other Orthodox churches, however, such as the Greek Orthodox church, the services continue to be in ancient Greek. The worship is based on liturgy which is centuries old. The most common is the liturgy of Saint John Chrysostom c.347–407 CE.

The most noticeable feature which distinguishes an Orthodox place of worship from a Roman Catholic church is the Iconostasis screen which hides the altar. The Iconostasis is covered with icons, holy paintings of saints. Orthodox Christians believe that pictures help them to meditate and to worship God prayerfully. The first thing they do as they enter the church is to light a candle and place it in front of an icon. They kiss the icon and make the sign of the cross.

In the centre of the iconostasis screen is a pair of doors which are open during the service to show that through Jesus people can reach God.

The mystical meditative approach to theology and worship is possibly the most distinctive feature of Orthodox Christianity. The worshippers try to achieve an inner stillness. It is expressed in these words of Saint Symeon from the tenth century.

I know that the Immovable comes down;
I know that the Invisible appears to me;
I know that he who is far outside the whole creation
Takes me into himself and hides me in his arms.

I know that I shall not die, for I am within the Life,
I have the whole of Life springing up as a fountain within me.
He is in my heart, he is in heaven.

SACRAMENTS AND RITES OF PASSAGE

The Roman Catholic Church has seven sacraments:

- The Eucharist
- Baptism
- Confirmation
- Marriage
- Reconciliation
- Ordination
- Anointing the Sick

The Orthodox Christian Churches have virtually the same sacraments as the Roman Catholic Church and also accept the definition given by Saint Augustine (354–430 CE) that a sacrament is 'the outward visible form of an inner invisible grace'. They call the sacraments the Holy Mysteries. The most important sacrament in both Churches is the Eucharist because both believe that it is a channel of grace to believers who receive the body and blood of Jesus in the bread and wine.

Baptism is important for both Roman Catholic and Orthodox Christians.

Orthodox babies are baptised by total immersion. The priest says, 'The servant of God (name of the baby) is baptised into the name of the Father, Amen. And of the Son, Amen. And of the Holy Spirit, Amen.' Immediately after baptism the baby is chrismated. Chrismation is a service in which the believer is anointed with oil. The priest anoints the baby with oil eight times on different parts of the body, saying, 'The seal of the gift of the Holy Spirit.' Chrismation is the equivalent of confirmation and so the child can take part in the Eucharist after chrismation.

The most distinctive difference in the Orthodox wedding service is the wearing of crowns by the couple who are getting married. The tradition goes back to the idea of martyrs' crowns. The couple are dedicating their lives to each other in front of God in the same way that martyrs gave their lives for their faith. In the Russian church the wedding crowns may be of silver or gold whilst in the Greek churches they may be made of leaves and flowers like those worn by victors in ancient sporting ceremonies, such as the Olympic games.

THE ROMAN CATHOLIC AND PROTESTANT SPLIT

In the sixteenth century a new division split the Christian Church in the West. It was the Protestant Reformation. The people who began the movement did not want to split the Church. They wanted to reform it. They protested about the beliefs and practices which they believed were not in line with the teaching in the New Testament. In particular, the reformers were protesting because the Church was so wealthy and politically powerful that some of the Church leaders had grown lazy and corrupt.

Not all the Church was corrupt of course. There were many devout Christians and religion was being taken very seriously all over Europe. That is why there were people who thought about making reforms. The protests had been going on since the previous century but 1517 was the year when matters came to a crisis point.

A monk called Martin Luther (1483–1546) was the Professor of Biblical Studies at Wittenberg, a small Saxon town in Germany. He had been lecturing on Paul's letter to the Romans in the New Testament. Romans chapter 5 is about Justification by Faith. This means that Christians are accepted by God because they believe in Jesus Christ. They are justified by their faith in Jesus. Salvation is a gift. People cannot earn their way into heaven by doing good deeds. People certainly cannot buy a place in heaven with money.

At the time Pope Leo X, a patron of artists such as Michelangelo and Raphael, was having improvements made to St Peter's in Rome. He expected his archbishops and bishops to help raise the money.

Various ways were being used to raise money. A Dominican friar, Johan Tetzel, was travelling the countryside selling indulgences. These were pardons from the Pope.

People could buy forgiveness not only for their own sins but for the sins of their dead relatives.

Martin Luther was appalled by the selling of indulgences and he decided to protest about everything that was a departure from Biblical Christianity. Martin Luther was also a parish priest so he reported his concerns to his superior, the Archbishop of Mainz, convinced that the Church would debate the issue. In those days one of the ways to challenge other people to join in a debate was to fasten your thesis to the church door with your personal dagger. Martin Luther's document contained not just one thesis but 95 theses.

Martin Luther never got the chance to have his debate in Wittenberg. The Archbishop of Mainz complained to Rome. Martin Luther was summoned to appear before a council at Augsburg, Germany. Luther refused to recant his beliefs. In 1519 he burnt a document from the Pope and in April 1521 Martin Luther was excommunicated at a council called the Diet of Worms. He was also made an outlaw by the Emperor Charles V.

Prince Frederick, the Elector of Saxony, had Luther kidnapped and imprisoned in a castle at Wartburg in order to protect him from being assassinated. Many of the princes in Germany and other European countries did not want the Pope in Italy to have so much influence on their national politics. They saw the Reformation as an opportunity to lessen the power of the Pope in their countries.

Whilst Luther was imprisoned he translated the Bible into German and wrote many pamphlets, articles and tracts. It was said that when Luther wrote anything, in two weeks it was read by the whole of Germany and in four weeks by Europe.

The Scala Santa is a staircase which was thought to have been brought by St Helena, Constantine's mother, from the ruins of Pilate's palace in Jerusalem. Jesus may have stood on this staircase so it is considered very holy. Just before the events of the Reformation, Martin Luther went on a pilgrimage to Rome. Ever since he was 22, when he had made a vow in a thunderstorm, he had tried to be a devout Christian. Now he was in his thirties and still religion had not brought him peace of mind. He went on his knees up the holy staircase begging forgiveness for his sins. Halfway up, he stopped. Suddenly he realised the truth of what he had been reading in Romans 5 about justification by faith not by works.

In 1530 the Confession of Augsberg was submitted to the Emperor as the basis for a Protestant Church.

Martin Luther ended his days quietly. He married an ex-nun, had several children and lived quietly at home studying and writing. The movement he had started led to the formation of Protestant Churches independent of the Pope in Germany, Norway, Sweden and Denmark. They are called Lutheran Churches.

There were other people who were influenced by Martin Luther but who felt that the Reformation needed to go even further.

John Calvin (1509–64), a French lawyer and theologian, believed, like Luther, that all true believers are priests and can pray directly to God for forgiveness of sins. Luther had no real desire to change the way the Church was organised. Calvin, however, thought churches should be organised in a more democratic manner. Worship was to be kept simple and no images were allowed in churches. Calvin also believed, like Luther, that the final authority for Christians is not the Church but the Bible. He believed that it is the duty of each Christian, by the guidance of the Holy Spirit, to interpret the Bible for himself or herself. In 1536 he brought out a book, *The Institutes of the Christian Religion*, that had a great effect on the Protestant Reformation. Calvin's book explained, by careful study of Biblical texts, all the key beliefs of Protestantism.

Calvin had studied Hebrew and Greek as well as Latin. He had also been influenced by Luther's German New Testament and by earlier reformers who had been translating the Bible. The invention of printing in the previous century had led to people such as William Tyndale getting Bibles printed in Europe and smuggled into England. The Bible had been in a Latin translation for centuries. Now there was the opportunity for it not only to be written in the languages of each country but to have it printed so that ordinary Christians all over Europe could read it for themselves and not have to rely on priests telling them what it meant. On the whole the early Protestants took the Bible literally. Some would only accept the truth of something if it was in the Bible and others would accept ideas as long as they did not contradict the principles of the Bible.

Calvin's influence led to the establishment of Reformed Churches in France, Germany, Holland and Hungary. His teachings had an influence on Puritan theologians in Britain too. In Scotland, a Roman Catholic priest, John Knox, defended the ideas of the Reformation. After imprisonment and exile in England and Europe, he returned to Scotland in 1559 and supervised the preparation of the constitution and liturgy of the reformed Church. The ministers were called Presbyters and Presbyterianism became the State Church in Scotland.

Another group, which had similar ideas to Calvin, had existed since the start of the Reformation. They were the Anabaptists who were baptising adult believers by full immersion because they had read about this in the Bible. Most of the adults had been baptised as children. Ana means again and Anabaptist means someone who has been baptised again. The ideas of this denomination continued through the Reformation and became the Baptist Churches. The first Baptist Church started in Holland in 1609 among some English exiles. In 1639 they took their beliefs to Rhode Island, North America. Many Baptists continue to hold Calvinist ideas.

It was obvious that reform was needed so the Roman Catholic Church had a Counter Reformation. The Council of Trent between 1545 and 1563 clarified the Roman Catholic doctrines but it also made many reforms which limited the nepotism (appointing relatives to influential positions in the Church), the luxurious living and the neglect of parish duties. There were many reforms which encouraged the establishing of schools and the training of clergy.

THE DIFFERENCES BETWEEN ROMAN CATHOLICS AND PROTESTANTS

THE AUTHORITY OF THE POPE

Roman Catholics believe that the most important person in the world is the Pope, who is God's representative on earth.

For a variety of reasons Protestants refuse to accept the authority of the Pope. Some emphasise the priesthood and equality of all believers.

THE VIRGIN MARY

Roman Catholics give a special place in their worship to the Virgin Mary, the mother of Jesus. They pray to her but they do not worship her. They also pray to the saints as intermediaries who will intercede for them to God. They believe that praying to Mary and to the saints makes it more likely that God will answer their prayers.

Protestants influenced by the teaching of John Calvin put great emphasis on the second of the Ten Commandments. This is the commandment not to make graven images. To many Protestant Christians, statues in church look like idolatry and superstition (see page 153). Many cathedrals in Britain have statues with broken heads somewhere inside or outside the building. This dates back to when the Puritan iconoclasts smashed the statues.

THE EUCHARIST

Martin Luther challenged the teaching of transubstantiation. This was an issue which theologians were debating at the time. The word transubstantiation was first used in the twelfth century and it means that the bread and wine had actually changed into the body and blood of Jesus. Transubstantiation was a miracle that happened at every mass. Luther believed that the body and blood are in with and under the elements of bread and wine. Luther's view is called Consubstantiation because it means that they are both things at once; they are still bread and wine but the body and blood of Jesus are also really present.

Some Protestants thought Luther's view was a compromise. They believed Jesus was present spiritually but they felt that it was superstitious magic to think of the bread and wine as anything more than symbols of the body and blood of Jesus. They felt that it was the faith of the believer that brought grace to the person's soul.

There are other differences between Roman Catholics and Protestants, for example Roman Catholic clergymen are not married, there is confession of sins which Roman Catholics must make at least once a year and there are different attitudes towards birth control and other ethical issues. None of these are as significant as the main issues which started at the time of the Reformation and remain a source of disagreement.

Protestant divisions did not stop at the time of the Reformation. Some of the later Protestant denominations found it even harder to tolerate Roman Catholic ideas and some even felt alienated from other Protestants.

THE REFORMATION IN ENGLAND

In the Reformation the situation in England was different from the rest of Europe. Some of the Church leaders were interested in the ideas of Luther but the king, Henry VIII (1509–47) would have nothing to do with the Reformation at first. He received the title 'Defender of the Faith' for his book attacking Luther. Then Henry had a disagreement with the Pope. Henry wanted to divorce his wife, Catherine of Aragon, so he could marry Anne Boleyn. The Pope, Leo X, would not give permission for the marriage to be annulled. Henry broke with Rome and made himself Head of the Church in England in 1534.

The Archbishop of Canterbury, Thomas Cranmer (1489–1556), wrote two prayer books in English. Previously, worship had been in Latin. It was even forbidden to say the Lord's Prayer in English. Cranmer's second prayer book became the basis for the Book of Common Prayer in 1662. This was used in the Church of England until the Alternative Service Book in 1980.

Queen Elizabeth I (1533–1603) had managed to survive the struggle between the Roman Catholics and the Protestants which raged through England after the death of Henry. She adopted Protestant doctrine on main issues but kept the church hierarchy and organisation of the Roman style. This may be why the Anglican Church seems to sit as a compromise between the two traditions. Today the Anglican Church is found all around the world. In Britain it is called the Church of England, the Episcopal Church in Scotland, the Church in Wales and the Church of Ireland.

In 1611 King James I of England (1603–25) authorised the printing of the Bible in English. This version is called the Authorised Version or the King James Version. It was the most commonly used Bible by English-speaking Protestants for the next three centuries.

PROTESTANT DIVISIONS

Protestants had split from the Roman Catholic Church because they did not accept the authority of the Pope. Some Protestants in England felt that the reforms had not gone far enough. They wanted to see less control by bishops and priests over the lay people.

The ordinary people in Christian Churches are called lay people or the laity. The word laity comes from 'laos', the Greek word for 'people'.

Some Protestant Christians felt that the lay people should have more say in the way their churches were run.

Some of the splits were caused by different opinions about doctrine based on teachings found in the Bible. They read about the first Christians in the New Testament and they felt that the early church was very democratic. They also felt that it was very dynamic because it was led by the Holy Spirit.

In England, Christians were expected to conform to the rules of the established church, the Church of England. At one time people who did not go to church on Sunday were fined. There was not only persecution of Roman Catholics, Jews and witches at various times but also the persecution of Protestant 'non-conformists'.

Some Protestants were Puritans who felt that the Church of England had not gone far enough in their reforms. They followed the teachings of John Calvin and wanted to abolish everything that suggested luxury and idolatry. Some Puritans broke away from the Church of England and some joined groups similar to the official Church of Scotland. In 1572 the first English Presbyterian Church was set up in London and in 1580 the first Congregational Church in Norwich.

Between 1620 and 1640 about 20,000 Puritans fled from England. They wanted freedom to worship according to their conscience. Among them were the Pilgrim Fathers who were banished to Holland and then sailed to America aboard the Mayflower in 1620. They established Congregationalism in New England.

Puritanism not only led to the founding of colonies in America but to civil war in England. Oliver Cromwell (1599–1658) was a convinced Calvinist. He led the Parliamentary side to victory in the English civil war against Charles I. Many Puritans did not want to get rid of the monarchy. They wanted to make sure that the ruler was not a Roman Catholic. When Cromwell died they supported the restoration of King Charles II.

In 1681 Charles II signed a charter giving a region in America to William Penn (1644–1718), in payment of a debt owed by the king to Penn's father, Admiral Sir William Penn. Unlike his father, William Penn was a Quaker. The region he governed, Pennsylvania, was one of the original American colonies. The new Quaker province was known for its fair treatment of the native Americans.

Quakers was a name given to The Society of Friends which was founded by George Fox in 1652. The nickname 'Quaker' was given to George Fox by Justice Bennett after Fox told the judge to 'tremble before the word of the Lord'. Fox spent a total of eight years in prison and 15,000 Quakers are said to have died for their faith between 1650 and the Toleration Act of 1689 when Protestant non-conformists were allowed freedom of worship. Members of the Society of Friends believe there is 'something of God' (according to Fox) in every person. This 'inner light' can be discovered in silent prayer.

Briggflatts Meeting House near Sedbergh, Yorkshire Dales.

A Quakers' *meeting in the 1800s.*

Friends have no clergy, renounce all formal church practices and meet in meeting houses like this one which is still in use in Brigflatts, Yorkshire.

In the seventeenth century Friends wore simple clothes similar to Puritans. They had broad brimmed hats which they refused to doff to anyone, believing all to be equal. They also called everyone 'thee' and 'thou'. These were the words used among family and friends instead of 'you'.

Quakers have always been pacifists and they continue to work throughout the world for peace.

PEACE TESTIMONY OF THE SOCIETY OF FRIENDS

(from a document presented to Charles II in 1660. The document had the title: A Declaration from the Harmless and Innocent People of God, called Quakers.)

We utterly deny all outward wars and strife, and fightings with outward weapons, for any end, or under any pretence whatever; this is our testimony to the whole world. The Spirit of Christ by which we are guided is not changeable, so as once to command us from a thing as evil, and again to move unto it; and we certainly know, and testify to the world, that the Spirit of Christ which leads us into all truth, will never move us to fight and war against any man with outward weapons, neither for the kingdom of Christ, nor for the kingdoms of the world.

In the eighteenth century two brothers, John and Charles Wesley, sons of a Church of England vicar, started a group in Oxford to pray and study the Bible seriously and methodically. John was already ordained. Among the group was another person who would have a great influence on parts of England, George Whitefield. They became known as 'the Holy Club' and by the nickname 'Methodists'. Their activities included visiting the sick and the poor and comforting prisoners, especially those who were going to be hanged. John Wesley was serious about religion but he could not find peace of mind. He went to America with Charles who was working in the administration of a new colony. John was to work as a missionary. When he found he was no good at the task, John returned to England in 1737 on a ship where he was impressed by the calmness of some German Moravian Christians during a storm. On Whit Sunday 1738 John Wesley had a conversion experience at a meeting where someone read Luther's preface to the Epistle to the Romans. Charles was back in England and living near by so John went to tell him about the news only to find that Charles was already writing a hymn about a similar experience. The Wesley brothers did not intend to break away from the Church of England; they wanted to reform it.

John Wesley's preaching appealed to the emotions of his listeners and many Anglican churches refused to let him preach. Wesley solved the problem by preaching in the open. He rode more than 300,000 miles (over 400,000 km) on horseback and preached more than 40,000 sermons.

He criticised the clergy for ignoring the poor. He created orphanages, schools, dispensaries for the poor who were sick and a lending fund so workmen did not need to pawn their tools in hard times. The day John Wesley wrote his last entry in his diary, he also wrote a letter. It was to William Wilberforce, encouraging him in his campaign against slavery.

John Wesley's rule

Do all the good you can,
By all the means you can,
In all the ways you can,
In all the places you can,
At all the times you can,
To all the people you can,
As long as ever you can.

John Wesley 1703–91

In 1784 John Wesley decided that instead of having a successor there should be one hundred preachers. In the same year the American War of Independence ended. All the Anglican clergy had fled from the rebel states and it was difficult for congregations to take communion. Wesley responded to a request for help from American Methodists. He ordained some presbyters to administer the sacraments.

John Wesley tried to avoid separation from the Church of England but it was inevitable. Under English law 'Dissenting' preachers and chapels had to be registered to avoid persecution. Eventually, in 1787 John Wesley advised that all Methodist preachers of the gospel and their places of meeting, which he called Methodist chapels, should be licensed. Methodists were later to be very influential in British politics, being involved in Trade Unions and the Liberal Party in the nineteenth century and the Labour Party in the twentieth century.

After the Industrial Revolution in England, people flocked to the towns from the countryside. There were many social problems and poverty in towns and cities and the established Churches seemed to be losing touch with the ordinary people. In 1861, a Methodist minister called William Booth was refused permission from the Methodists to become a travelling evangelist. He left the Methodists and started a new evangelistic movement called the Salvation Army. Members wear uniforms and are organised like an army because Christians are like soldiers fighting evils in society. They saw the dangers of alcoholism among the poor and made a total ban on alcohol among their members. The Salvation Army meet in citadels. They preach in the cities because that is where they find the people who need them. The music of the Salvation Army band is to witness to their faith and to worship God but also to attract followers. The Salvation Army worked among the poor from the very beginning and continue to do so today. They also help people who are homeless and try to trace lost persons.

ICT FOR RESEARCH

Look up the Salvation Army website to see the range of their activities.

By the start of the twentieth century most cities had a range of gospel halls as well as churches, chapels and other Christian buildings.

Pentecostal Churches such as The Assemblies of God and the Elim Church are one of the largest growing types of Christian Churches in the developing countries. These Churches emphasise spiritual gifts from the Holy Spirit such as healing and speaking with tongues like the early Christians.

In the United Kingdom fewer people go to church than in the past. In 1972 some Congregational and Presbyterian Churches united to become the United Reform Church in England and Wales. This union was not only because of falling numbers. It was a logical combination because these two Protestant Churches had common beliefs from the beginning.

THE JEWISH BACKGROUND TO CHRISTIANITY

The Jews had one Temple. It was in Jerusalem. When Jesus was a baby, he was circumcised and named on the eighth day in accordance with Jewish tradition. Luke 2:21–38 tells how Jesus was taken to the Temple 'to present him to the Lord' like the dedication of Samuel in the Jewish Scriptures (1 Samuel 1:26–28). The visit was required by Jewish religious law to make the offering for the purification of his mother, Mary, after childbirth. In Leviticus 12:6–8 are the rules about the offerings to be made. Poor families could offer two doves instead of a lamb and this is what Mary did.

Jesus was brought up as a Jew in Nazareth in Palestine. When he was 12 he went with his parents to Jerusalem to celebrate the Passover. Jesus must have visited Jerusalem many times afterwards because there were three annual pilgrimage festivals when Jews visited the Temple.

Every town and village in Palestine had at least one synagogue. The word is from the Greek for meeting together. The synagogue services included prayers, readings from the Torah scrolls which were written in Hebrew and a sermon in the local language, which was Aramaic (a slightly more modern form of Hebrew). There were elders in charge of the synagogue. Any male Jew could be invited to give the sermon. Jesus was asked to do this sometimes (e.g. Mark 1:21; Mark 6:1–6). In his teachings he was always quoting the Jewish Scriptures. 'Love God' and 'Love your neighbour' are both teachings from the Jewish Scriptures.

Jesus kept the Jewish Law and his teaching in the Sermon on the Mount (Matthew chapters 5–7) (see pages 22–29) makes it clear that he had no intention of destroying the Law. Jesus believed in keeping the spirit of the Law not just the letter of the Law. When Jesus healed people on the Sabbath his critics said he was working and therefore breaking the Sabbath. Jesus replied that, 'The Sabbath was made for man, not man for the Sabbath' (Mark 2:27).

During the last week of his life, Jesus was in Jerusalem and most days he was preaching in the Temple courtyards. On the Thursday night he had a last meal with his disciples. The Jewish Passover has not changed for thousands of years. Historians debate whether or not the Thursday meal was the actual Passover meal that year but the Passover was definitely in the minds of all present. It was certainly in the minds of the gospel writers when they described the meal. Jesus followed the usual pattern of a Jewish meal by blessing the bread, breaking it and passing it round. This shows that all the people at the meal share in the blessing. When Jesus took the cup he said, 'This is the blood of the covenant which is poured out for many' (Mark 14:24). In these words, Christians see a reference to a prophecy in the Jewish Scriptures. In Jeremiah 31:31–34, the prophet Jeremiah talks of a New Covenant where the Jewish Law will be written not on stone but on the hearts of all the people. Christians call their scriptures the New Testament or New Covenant. They also read the Jewish Scriptures which they call the Old Testament because they need to understand the continuity of their faith from its Jewish background.

ECUMENISM

Ecumenism is the name given to the movement which tries to unite Christians. The adjective 'ecumenical' comes from the Greek oikou menikos which means 'of the inhabited earth'.

There have been several attempts to bring together the different Christian denominations into one Church.

In 1910, 1,200 delegates of the world Protestant churches met at Edinburgh for the World Missionary Conference. Their aim was to stop competing with each other for new converts in the colonies and countries that were open to missionaries. This meeting is often quoted as the first step taken towards Christian reunion.

The ecumenical movement began after the First World War and culminated in a meeting in 1937 which recommended the formation of a World Council of Churches but work was interrupted by the Second World War. The British Council of Churches was formed in 1942. It was made up at first of Anglican and Protestant British Churches and some interdenominational movements like the YMCA.

In 1948 the World Council of Churches (WCC) was formed as 'a fellowship of Churches which accepts our Lord Jesus Christ as God and Saviour'.

The assembly of the WCC meets about every six years in varied locations around the world. In 1960 at St Andrews in Scotland the World Council's central committee unanimously accepted an expanded draft of the basis of faith, mainly at the request of Orthodox members:

The World Council of Churches is a community of churches which confess the Lord Jesus Christ, according to the Holy Scriptures, as God and Saviour and therefore seek to fulfil that to which they are jointly called, to the glory of God the Father, the Son and the Holy Spirit.

The work of the WCC is divided into three parts:

The badge of the World Council of Churches. The ship is an ancient Christian symbol representing the church in the world.

- church relations
- ecumenical study and promotion
- inter-church aid and service to refugees.

In 2002 there were 342 Churches in more than 120 countries on all continents as members of the WCC. This represents about 400 million Christians, mostly of the Protestant and Orthodox traditions. The Southern Baptists of the United States are non-members of the WCC. As yet the Roman Catholic Church has not become a member but the other traditions try not to make decisions which would exclude this possibility. The Roman Catholic Church itself has been working towards healing the problems which have resulted from the past history of Christianity. These moves towards reconciliation and mutual understanding are not only involving discussions with other Christians but with other faiths. Ever since the second Vatican Council (1962–65) the Roman Catholic Church has been trying to make changes which will help the Church to be a good influence in the modern world. In recent years, the Pope has apologised on behalf of the Roman Catholic Church for persecutions such as the Inquisition and for not doing more to help the Jews during the Holocaust.

Part of the inspiration for ecumenism comes from the example of some of the Christian Churches in the developing nations. These were once called the younger churches but are now often called Asian or African churches.

Christians in Europe saw the freshness of the faith of the new Churches, their courage in the face of persecution and were reminded of the New Testament gospel.

Three Christian Churches in South India joined together in 1947. This is their badge.

ICT FOR RESEARCH

Look up 'South India, church of' in an encyclopaedia such as Britannica.

Which Christian denominations were involved?

What beliefs did they feel that they could hold in common?

Was uniformity in church services essential?

What reactions did they get from other Christians around the world?

Not all Christians welcome ecumenism and some have mixed feelings about the movement. The main fears are that:

- it could dilute the truth of the gospel

- it could lose the teachings which are special to particular denominations
- it might even create another version of Christianity.

Some Christians think that meeting to discuss differences between denominations is simply a waste of time and that Christians should work together to do something practical. They feel there is no need for Churches to have uniformity in the way they do anything. The important thing, they feel, is to recognise that as Christians they already have a basic unity.

Ecumenism is not about making all Churches be the same but it is about obeying the command of Jesus to love one another.

As Paul said to the Christians of Ephesus in the first century of the Christian era:

> *Be kind and compassionate to one another, forgiving each other, just as in Christ God forgave you.*
>
> (Ephesians 4:32)

TAIZÉ

Taizé is a Christian community in a small village in France. It was founded by Brother Roger Schutz in 1940. He was 25 years old and it was wartime. He began to offer hospitality to refugees, particularly Jews escaping from Nazi Germany. After two years his first brothers joined him. Today there are more than 100 brothers mainly of various Protestant denominations from 25 countries. Small groups of brothers also work overseas among the poor in Asia, Africa and Latin America.

After the war, Brother Roger encouraged the overcoming of hatred between French and Germans. Reconciling Protestants and Roman Catholics was another main concern.

Other ecumenical centres include:

- Iona, a holy island and place of pilgrimage since St Columba went there in 563 CE. The community was founded by George Macleod in 1938.

- Corrymeela at Ballycastle in County Antrim, Northern Ireland. It was founded in 1965 by Christians, both Roman Catholics and Protestants.
- Coventry Cathedral and the Community of the Cross of Nails.

Ecumenism is not only about communities like Taizé working for reconciliation and councils of Church leaders discussing unity. Ecumenism also exists on a local level.

FOR DISCUSSION

Can you think of any examples in your area where there is cooperation between Churches for some community project?

Has there been a big evangelistic campaign?

Are there any shared churches or joint prayer meetings?

Some Christians say that the past should be forgotten and the Church should start again. Others say the issue is not about forgetting but about forgiving. What do you think?

Reconciliation is a word often used when talking about places like Taizé. It comes from the following passage about the ministry of Reconciliation. It shows that Christians who work towards peace believe that it is at the heart of the Christian gospel.

Therefore if anyone is in Christ, he is a new creation, the old has gone, the new has come! All this is from God, who reconciled us to himself through Christ and gave us the ministry of reconciliation: that God was reconciling the world to himself in Christ, not counting men's sins against them. And he has committed to us the message of reconciliation. We are therefore Christ's ambassadors, as though God were making his appeal through us. We implore you on Christ's behalf: Be reconciled to God. God made him who had no sin to be sin for us, so that in him we might become the righteousness of God.

(2 Corinthians 5:17–21)

FOR DISCUSSION

'The church today is closer to the early Christians than at any other time in history.'

THE CHARISMATIC MOVEMENT

The name 'charismatic movement' comes from the Greek for gifts, 'charismata'.

The power of the Holy Spirit, according to the New Testament, inspires people and gives special charismatic gifts, such as the ability to preach, teach, heal, prophesy and speak in tongues like the disciples did after Pentecost. Most important of all, the Holy Spirit helps them to spread love in the world. 'The fruit of the Spirit is love, joy, peace, patience, kindness, goodness, faithfulness, gentleness and self-control.' (Galatians 5:22).

Many churches in the traditional denominations such as the Anglican Church and the Roman Catholic Church have been affected by the charismatic movement.

LIBERATION THEOLOGY

In the last century, many Roman Catholic priests became very concerned about the inequality and exploitation in many developing countries but things came to a head in South America. Some priests found they were struggling against their own Church as well as the governments in their struggle for justice for the poor.

They live and work among the poor to empower them. They are prepared to work alongside Communists and non-Christians to:

- empower the poor
- assist them to educate themselves
- find self-help alternatives.

Camillo Torres was a Columbian priest who took part in armed uprisings and insisted that the Catholic who is not a revolutionary is living in mortal sin. He was shot dead in 1966.

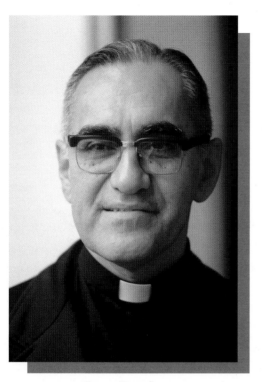

Oscar Romero

Oscar Romero (1917–80) was ordained Bishop of El Salvador in 1970.

Another priest, a close friend of Romero, called Rutilo Grande, was killed by government forces for his outspoken opposition to the country's politics.

Romero preached sermons every Sunday which were broadcast on the radio. These were very critical of the way in which the poor were treated. He opposed violence but encouraged poor people to organise in order to oppose the government. In March 1980 he himself was killed while celebrating mass.

His death had a great impact on El Salvador and on the whole of the Roman Catholic Church. In Latin America he is often referred to as 'St Romero of the Americas'.

AIMS AND APPROACHES

Vatican II encouraged Catholics into new ways of thinking about things like poverty and social injustice.

Some Catholic theologians began exploring the idea of life as a pilgrimage of hope, an evolution towards better things. They believe that Christians should no longer be content with putting up with their sufferings patiently and waiting for the promise of heaven when they die. Jesus favoured the poor and oppressed and they think that Christians today should do the same.

Liberation Theologians draw on the Bible for examples of God helping people oppose the power of the enemy, slavery and political and social discrimination.

These include the Exodus from Egypt when Moses led the Hebrew slaves to freedom, the return of the Israelites from exile in Babylon and the struggle against the Greeks led by Judas the Maccabee. These events have become symbols for those trying to free people from slavery and oppression.

Liberation Theologians have often been accused of being Marxist in their teachings. They say that to adopt some of the good parts of Marxist theory does not mean that they share Marxist views about religion.

PRACTICE EXAMINATION QUESTIONS

1 (a) **Describe two ways that Christians from different Churches and denominations try to work together. (*8 marks*)**

There are many possible ways that Christians of different denominations might try to work together. Small local efforts to unite for campaigns and for charity or community activities are as acceptable as large scale international festivals and the work of ecumenical centres of reconciliation. Good descriptions do not have to be very long to be effective. State the short- or long-term purposes of the effort, where and when the joint work might occur and which groups might be involved. The two examples can be similar or different in scale or purpose.

(b) **Explain why the three main Christian groups are called 'Roman Catholic', 'Orthodox' and 'Protestant'. (*7 marks*)**

Whole books have been written on small parts of this topic. The question does not expect a long thesis about the three main branches of Christianity. You are expected to show that you understand why the names are appropriate for each of the three. Briefly you might explain the historical context of the main splits, for example a few sentences about the ancient Church of Rome, the Great Schism of 1054 and the Protestant Reformation.

(c) **'Christianity has caused more problems than it has solved.'**
Do you agree? Give reasons to support your answer and show that you have thought about different points of view. (*5 marks*)

Christianity has had such a long history that it is not surprising that there have been shameful events for which even the Pope has apologised. Remember that you should try to present a balanced argument. Notice the word 'more' in the question.

2 (a) **Describe the main differences between Roman Catholic and Protestant Christians. (*8 marks*)**

There are many equally valid ways of approaching this question. The main differences stem from the Reformation so some account of the original split might be helpful as a starting point but remember that this is not a history examination. Select some areas where everybody acknowledges there are differences. For example, you might describe attitudes to sources of authority such as the Pope, the Church and the Bible and differing theological emphases about Mary or the Eucharist, etc.

(b) **Explain the importance of the Charismatic movement for some Christians. (*7 marks*)**

The answer might cover some Christians from one particular denomination, Pentecostal, Anglican, or Roman Catholic, for example, where there has been charismatic ministry or may deal with Christians in general.

It might be sensible to begin by showing that you understand what is meant by the Charismatic movement. Descriptions of the phenomena shown in charismatic worship are relevant but they are not likely to be the main focus of a good answer. A competent explanation of the importance might consider the effects that Christians believe the gifts and power of the Holy Spirit can have on their lives.

(c) **'Christians share many of the same beliefs so they should forget their differences.'**
Do you agree? Give reasons to support your answer and show that you have thought about different points of view. (*5 marks*)

Remember to support your opinions with reasons and, when considering other points of view, think what various Christian denominations might say. Unity is desirable but the issue is not a simple matter. Differences in beliefs and practices are often based on matters of principle.

3 (a) **Describe one example of ecumenism in Christianity. (*8 marks*)**

Taizé might be used as an example but any attempt to build bridges rather than barriers between

Christian denominations could be described. Good descriptions tend to give information which addresses: When?; Where?; Who?; What? and Why? A description might state why something was done but developed explanations tend to belong to the parts of a question which test your understanding of significance, importance, meaning or application. This is a helpful point to remember when you are planning answers.

(b) Explain why Christians might support ecumenism. (7 marks)

If you have not already given a definition of ecumenism, you might use one to introduce your explanation. You may feel that you need to distinguish between uniformity and unity. For what reasons might Christians want unity? Why might they not want divisions? Think of Biblical teachings. Try not to waffle. Does 'support' include doing something practical?

(c) 'Ecumenism is the most important issue for Christians today.'

Do you agree? Give reasons to support your answer and show that you have thought about different points of view. (5 marks)

There are a number of equally valid ways to approach this discussion. You might develop points you have made earlier to show why some Christians support ecumenism and think it is important. Even they, however, may not think it is the most important issue. For example, they may for various reasons, think Liberation Theology is the most important issue.

4 (a) Describe the main beliefs about Jesus of Nazareth which are common to Roman Catholic, Orthodox and Protestant Christians. (8 marks)

You are not expected to know every single belief about Jesus. The question wants you to identify the main beliefs held in common by most Christians. You may wish to quote the beliefs about Jesus from the earliest creeds or write about the basic gospel teaching of the early Christians. See Chapter 1 for the beliefs of Christians.

(b) Explain three differences between Roman Catholics and Orthodox Christians. (7 marks)

Try to choose things which are important or significant enough for you to develop your explanation and show that you understand the differences. Always look again at the question to see if you are required to write about beliefs or about practices. This particular question leaves it open so you may use anything.

(c) 'The Church today is closer to the early Christians than at any other time in history.'

Do you agree? Give reasons to support your answer and show that you have thought about different points of view. (5 marks)

You are being asked to think about the Church today and about the early Christians in the light of what you have written. Any sensible interpretation of a stimulus quotation is acceptable and there are many possible approaches to this question. You may wish to discuss the extent to which divisions have changed Christianity beyond recognition from its origins. You may feel that the splits are beginning to be healed as Christians try to look back to the early Christian Church and then forward to a positive future in which Christians stress their similarities rather than their differences. Your studies may have aroused your interest in some particular aspect of modern Christianity such as the Charismatic Movement or Liberation theology which might be made relevant to your discussion.

4

PILGRIMAGE

A pilgrimage is journey which people make to a special place.

Some people might say that they were making a pilgrimage if they went to see the home of a pop or movie star or to a special football ground.

However, when we are talking about religion, a pilgrimage is usually seen as a journey to a particular holy place made for religious reasons.

In Islam, pilgrimage to Makkah, the Hajj, is one of the duties which Muslims must try to undertake at least once in their lifetime. Some Hindus make many pilgrimages to particular places which are important in their religion.

When the Temple was still standing in Jerusalem, Jews tried to make three pilgrimages a year there to celebrate the three harvests of Pesach, Shavuot and Sukkot.

THINKING POINT

What sort of place would you like to make a pilgrimage to?

Think about why it would be important for you to go to this place.

There are no special rules about pilgrimage in Christianity though, over its 2000-year history, many people have made pilgrimages to particular places both in the Holy Land and in Europe.

People make these pilgrimages for many different reasons. Some go just to see the places where Jesus was or to see particular churches associated with special people or events. Some people go on pilgrimages to strengthen their faith and help them to feel closer to God.

Some places, such as Lourdes, are associated with healing miracles and people visit there in the hope of a cure, either for themselves, or for people who are close to them.

In the past, many people went on pilgrimages because they believed that making a special journey to a particular place would gain the indulgences. The idea of an indulgence was that it would prevent you having to stay too long in Purgatory when you died (see page 66).

FOR DISCUSSION

Find out more about indulgences and why Martin Luther was so opposed to them being used.

The very first Christian pilgrim that we know anything about was St Helena (c.248–328 CE), the wife of the Roman Emperor Constantinus Chlorus and the mother of Constantine the Great. Under the influence of her son she became a Christian. After a major family tragedy Helena made a pilgrimage to the Holy Land and ordered the building of churches on the traditional sites of the Nativity and the Ascension.

According to legend, she also found the buried remains of the cross on which Jesus was crucified and brought pieces of it back to Europe.

Next is a Spanish nun called Etheria. She wrote an account of her journeys for her colleagues at home, probably towards the end of the fourth century CE. This is known as Peregrinatio Etheriae or the Pilgrimage of Etheria. She describes her visits to places which appear in the Old and the New Testaments in Egypt, Palestine and Syria. In particular she gives a detailed account of worship in the early church in Jerusalem at this time.

ICT FOR RESEARCH

Try to find out more about St Helena and her discovery of the cross of Jesus.

PLACES OF PILGRIMAGE

BETHLEHEM

Bethlehem is about 8 km (5 miles) from Jerusalem and is believed to have been the birthplace of Jesus.

The first mention of Bethlehem in the Bible is when Rachel, the wife of Jacob and mother of Joseph, dies there:

> So Rachel died and was buried on the way to Ephrath (that is, Bethlehem). Over her tomb Jacob set up a pillar, and to this day that pillar marks Rachel's tomb.
> (Genesis 35:19–20)

The story in the Book of Ruth takes place in Bethlehem and it is where David is thought to have been born and where he was anointed King of Israel.

According to the Old Testament, the Messiah would come from Bethlehem:

> But you, Bethlehem Ephrathah,
> though you are small among the clans of Judah,
> out of you will come for me
> one who will be ruler over Israel,
> whose origins are from of old,
> from ancient times.
> (Micah 5:2)

In the New Testament, it of course appears as the birthplace of Jesus:

> So Joseph also went up from the town of Nazareth in Galilee to Judea, to Bethlehem in the town of David, because he belonged to the house and line of David. He went there to register with Mary, who was pledged to be married to him and was expecting a child. While they were there, the time came for the baby to be born, and she gave birth to her firstborn, a son. She wrapped him in cloths and placed him in a manger, because there was no room for them in the inn. (Luke 2:4–7)

> After Jesus was born in Bethlehem in Judea, during the time of King Herod, Magi from the East came to Jerusalem and asked, 'Where is the one who has been born king of the Jews? We saw his star in the East and have come to worship him.'

> When King Herod heard this he was disturbed, and all Jerusalem with him. When he had called together all the people's chief priests and teachers of the law, he asked them where the Christ was to be born. 'In Bethlehem in Judea,' they replied, 'for this is what the prophet has written:

> '"But you, Bethlehem, in the land of Judah,
> are by no means least among the rulers of Judah;
> for out of you will come a ruler
> who will be the shepherd of my people Israel."'
> (Matthew 2:1–6)

The exact place where Jesus was born was said by Justin Martyr, in the second century, to be a 'cave close to the village'. This cave is now under the Church of the Nativity which was originally built by

St Helena and later rebuilt by the Emperor Justinian between 527 and 565 CE. This is one of the oldest churches in existence.

In the fifth century, St Jerome built a monastery there and translated the Old Testament into Latin from the original Hebrew. This, together with the translation of the New Testament from Greek into Latin, which he had carried out earlier, forms the Vulgate Bible which is the standard used by the Roman Catholic Church.

Bethlehem now has many churches, convents, schools and hospitals funded by Christians from all over the world.

THINKING POINT

Try to find more information about Bethlehem and what it is like today.

NAZARETH

Nazareth is a city in Lower Galilee, northern Israel and is the traditional boyhood home of Jesus and where he preached a sermon in the synagogue.

There is no mention of Nazareth in the Old Testament and the first references in the New Testament are in gospel accounts of Jesus' birth.

> So Joseph also went up from the town of Nazareth in Galilee to Judea, to Bethlehem the town of David, because he belonged to the house and line of David.
>
> (Luke 2:4)

And then in the gospel of John:

> The next day Jesus decided to leave for Galilee. Finding Philip, he said to him, 'Follow me.'
>
> Philip, like Andrew and Peter, was from the town of Bethsaida. Philip found Nathanael and told him, 'We have found the one Moses wrote about in the Law, and about whom the prophets also wrote – Jesus of Nazareth, the son of Joseph.'
>
> 'Nazareth! Can anything good come from there?' Nathanael asked.
>
> 'Come and see,' said Philip   (John 1:43–46)

The only place in Nazareth which can be proved to date from the time of Jesus is the well which is called St Mary's Well.

Nazareth has many churches. The best known is the Roman Catholic Church of the Annunciation which was rebuilt in 1966. Here is the Grotto of the Annunciation, said to be where the Archangel Gabriel appeared to the Virgin Mary and told her that she was to be the mother of Jesus.

The Grotto of the Annunciation, Nazareth.

> In the sixth month, God sent the angel Gabriel to Nazareth, a town in Galilee, to a virgin pledged to be married to a man named Joseph, a descendant of David. The virgin's name was Mary. The angel went to her and said, 'Greetings, you who are highly favoured! The Lord is with you.'
>
> Mary was greatly troubled at his words and wondered what kind of greeting this might be. But the angel said to her, 'Do not be afraid, Mary, you have found favour with God. You will be with child and give birth to a son, and you are to give him the name Jesus. He will be great and will be called the Son of the Most High. The Lord God will give him the throne of his father David, and he will reign over the house of Jacob for ever; his kingdom will never end.'   (Luke 1:26–33)

Gabriel's Church is a Greek Catholic church which is also believed to be the site of the Annunciation.

The Synagogue Church is built on the traditional site of where Jesus preached:

> *He went to Nazareth, where he had been brought up, and on the Sabbath day he went into the synagogue, as was his custom. And he stood up to read. The scroll of the prophet Isaiah was handed to him. Unrolling it, he found the place where it is written:*
>
> *'The Spirit of the Lord is on me,*
> *because he has anointed me*
> *to preach good news to the poor.*
> *He has sent me to proclaim freedom for the prisoners*
> *and recovery of sight for the blind,*
> *to release the oppressed,*
> *to proclaim the year of the Lord's favour.'*
>
> *Then he rolled up the scroll, gave it back to the attendant and sat down. The eyes of everyone in the synagogue were fastened on him, and he began by saying to them, 'Today this scripture is fulfilled in your hearing...'*
>
> *All the people in the synagogue were furious when they heard this. They got up, drove him out of the town, and took him to the brow of the hill on which the town was built, in order to throw him down the cliff. But he walked right through the crowd and went on his way.*
> (Luke 4:16:21, 28–30)

The Church of Joseph stands on what is believed to be the site of Joseph's carpentry shop. The Mensa Christi, 'Table of Christ' Church, is where tradition says that Jesus dined with the Apostles after his Resurrection.

> *But after I have risen, I will go ahead of you into Galilee.*
> (Matthew 26:32)

Finally, the Basilica of Jesus the adolescent is on a hill above the city.

GALILEE

Galilee is in the extreme north of ancient Palestine and is divided into two parts, Upper and Lower. Upper Galilee is more mountainous than the lower area.

It appears in the Book of Judges as an area where Jews and Canaanites lived together.

Later, during the tenth century BCE, David and Solomon ruled Galilee and it became part of the northern kingdom.

It is an important area for Christians as Nazareth is the chief city of Lower Galilee and it is the area in which Jesus did most of his teaching.

> *Jesus went throughout Galilee, teaching in their synagogues, preaching the good news of the kingdom, and healing every disease and sickness among the people. News about him spread all over Syria, and people brought to him all who were ill with various diseases, those suffering severe pain, the demon-possessed, those having seizures, and the paralysed, and he healed them. Large crowds from Galilee, the Decapolis, Jerusalem, Judea and the region across the Jordan followed him.* (Matthew 4:23–25)

ICT FOR RESEARCH

Use an online Bible such as http://bible.gospelcom.net/ and find out just how much of Jesus' teaching took place in Galilee.

JERUSALEM

Jerusalem is a holy city for three religions. The Temple of the Jews stood on the Temple Mount in Jerusalem until it was destroyed by the Romans in 70 CE. Today all that remains is part of the foundation wall of the Temple and, known as the Western or 'Wailing' Wall, this is visited by many thousands of Jews every year.

It was this Temple which Jesus visited with his parents shortly after he was born:

> *When the time of their purification according to the Law of Moses had been completed, Joseph and Mary took him to Jerusalem to present him to the Lord (as it is written in the Law of the Lord), 'Every firstborn male is to be consecrated to the Lord', and to offer a sacrifice in keeping with what is said in the Law of the Lord: 'a pair of doves or two young pigeons'.* (Luke 2:22–24)

And also when he was 12:

> *Every year his parents went to Jerusalem for the Feast of the Passover. When he was twelve years old, they went up to the Feast, according to the custom. After the Feast was over, while his parents were returning home, the boy Jesus stayed behind in Jerusalem, but they were unaware of it. Thinking he was in their company, they travelled on for a day. Then they began looking for him among their relatives and friends. When they did not find him, they went back to Jerusalem to look for him. After three days they found him in the temple courts, sitting among the teachers, listening to them and asking them questions. Everyone who heard him was amazed at his understanding and his answers. When his parents saw him, they were astonished. His mother said to him, 'Son, why have you treated us like this? Your father and I have been anxiously searching for you.'*
>
> *'Why were you searching for me?' he asked. 'Didn't you know I had to be in my Father's house?' But they did not understand what he was saying to them.*
>
> (Luke 2:41–50)

The Wailing Wall, Jerusalem.

In the week before he was crucified, it was here that Jews threw out the money-changers:

> *On reaching Jerusalem, Jesus entered the temple area and began driving out those who were buying and selling there. He overturned the tables of the money-changers and the benches of those selling doves, and would not allow anyone to carry merchandise through the temple courts. And as he taught them, he said, 'Is it not written:*
>
> *"My house will be called a house of prayer for all nations"? But you have made it "a den of robbers".'*
>
> (Mark 11:15–17)

Following the destruction of the Temple, the Muslim Dome of the Rock was built on the Temple Mount. For Muslims this represents the place where Ibrahim prepared to sacrifice his son Ishmail and also from where the Prophet Muhammad ﷺ ascended through the seven heavens after his night journey from Makkah.

For each of these three religions it represents the earthly version of the heavenly Jerusalem. The city is full of synagogues, mosques and churches.

The name Jerusalem means 'Foundation of Shalem' (God). One of the first mentions of Jerusalem in the Bible is when Abram meets Melchizedek.

> *Then Melchizedek king of Salem (Jerusalem) brought out bread and wine. He was priest of God Most High, and he blessed Abram . . .*   (Genesis 14:18–19a)

In about 1000 BCE Jerusalem was captured by David and became the capital of his kingdom. Solomon later expanded the city and built the first Temple.

In 587–586 BCE the city and the Temple were destroyed by Nebuchadrezzar. It was not rebuilt until 515 BCE.

At the time of Jesus, the Holy Land was under Roman rule. Pompey captured the city in 63 BCE. In 40 BCE Herod the Great, a Jew, was created King of Judea by the Roman senate.

Herod was king for 36 years and rebuilt the Temple, including the Western Wall.

After Herod's death his son, Archelaus, took the throne but was deposed by the Romans who now appointed procurators to run the city. It was the fifth procurator, Pontius Pilate, who put Jesus to death.

Within Jerusalem there are many Christian groups:

- the Eastern Orthodox who have three resident patriarchs there
- Monophysites – Christians who believe that Jesus was divine and not human. These include the Abyssinian, Armenian and Coptic Churches. Most of these priests live around the Cathedral of St James
- Roman Catholic
- Protestant.

Six different Christian denominations have control over the Church of the Holy Sepulchure which is said to be built over the cave where Jesus' body was placed after his death: the Armenian Church, the Coptic Church, the Ethiopian Church, the Greek Orthodox Church, the Roman Catholic Church and the Syrian Church.

Other Christians believe that Jesus' body was placed in the Garden Tomb which is on the Mount of Olives.

Following the visit of Helena to Jerusalem, church building continued and in the sixth century Justinian rebuilt the Church of the Resurrection and many others.

Many of the important churches in Jerusalem were built by Justinian and later rebuilt by the crusaders. These include the Church of the Holy Sepulchre, the Church of St Anne (Mary's mother), the Armenian Cathedral of St James, and the Tomb of the Virgin.

St. Peter's Basilica, Rome.

THINKING POINT

Why do you think Jerusalem has become such an important place for so many people?

Find a map of Jerusalem and mark on it as many places as you can from this section so that you can see the relationship between them.

The Church of St Stephen, in the north of the city, was built by the Byzantine empress Eudocia, and the great Church of St Mary on the Temple hill, was built by Justinian.

Christian pilgrims may also visit the Mount of Olives where Jesus prayed with his disciples on Maundy Thursday, the Upper Room which is a later building supposedly standing on the site of the Last Supper, and also the Via Dolorosa, the route which Jesus took, carrying his cross, from the city to Golgotha where he was executed.

ROME

Rome has always been the centre of the Christian Church in the West and many people go there on pilgrimage.

There are seven great (maggiore) basilicas in Rome: St Peter's, S. Paolo Fuori le Mura (St Paul's Outside the Walls), and S. Giovanni in Laterano, S. Lorenzo Fuori le Mura (St Lawrence Outside the Walls), Sta Croce in Gerusalemme (Holy Cross in Jerusalem), S. Pietro in Vincoli (St Peter in Chains), and Sta. Maria Maggiore.

ST PETER'S

The city of Rome has a separate area within it called the Vatican City and it is here where the Pope, the head of the Roman Catholic Church, lives. It is also the site of the St Peter's Basilica. The basilica is protected by the fortified Castel Sant'Angelo.

This huge church stands on the site of an earlier Basilica built by Constantine. This was pulled down in 1506 by Pope Julius II to build a new church. Many architects and artists worked on the building which was not completed until 1677.

Legend says that St Peter was crucified in Rome and that he is buried under the altar of the church.

S. PAOLO FUORI LE MURA
(ST PAUL OUTSIDE THE WALLS)

There is a legend that St Paul was put to death in Rome during the Christian persecutions of 64 CE. Because he was a Roman citizen he would have been beheaded outside the walls of the city. His body is thought to have been buried under the church of St Paul. The original church was replaced in 386 CE and rebuilt in 1823.

There is a monastery, built on the traditional site of his death, three miles outside Rome.

S. GIOVANNI IN LATERANO
(ST JOHN LATERAN)

The original church was damaged by the Vandals in the fifth century, an earthquake and two fires before being rebuilt again from 1646 to 1650. Inside are relics of the heads of St Peter and St Paul. Here are the Scala Santa – the Holy Stairs. Legend, probably incorrectly, says that these were brought to Rome by Helena and were the stairs from Pilate's Palace so Jesus would have walked on them. They now have a wooden cover and pilgrims can climb them on their knees.

S. LORENZO FUORI LE MURA
(ST LAWRENCE OUTSIDE THE WALLS)

Dating from the fourth century it was rebuilt by Pope Honorius III in the thirteenth century.

STA. CROCE IN GERUSALEMME
(HOLY CROSS IN JERUSALEM)

This church houses the relic of the True Cross which Helena brought back from Jerusalem.

S. PIETRO IN VINCOLI
(ST PETER IN CHAINS)

This was built from 432 to 440 CE by the order of the Empress Eudoxia for the relics of the chains which St Peter wore in prison in Jerusalem. Later the chains used on him in Rome were added.

STA. MARIA MAGGIORE

Sta. Maria Maggiore was built in 432 CE and was the first great church in Rome dedicated to Mary.

Other important churches and pilgrimage sites are:

STA. MARIA DELLA VITTORIA
(ST MARY OF VICTORIES)

Built from 1605–26 this is best known for the painting by Bernini of the 'Ecstasy of St Teresa' (1645–52).

GESÙ

This church was built from 1568 to 1584 and is the mother church of the Society of Jesus (Jesuits).

S. AGOSTINO

Built from 1479 to 1483 this church is frequently visited by women hoping to become mothers. They pray here and leave offerings when their prayers are answered.

S. PIETRO IN MONTORIO

In the courtyard of this church is the Tempietto. This is a small chapel said to be built over the place where St Peter was crucified.

FOR DISCUSSION

Many of the churches in Rome have important relics in them. Try to find out more about some of these relics and the practice of venerating relics.

Do you think it might cause harm to a religion if a relic is proved not to be genuine?

LOURDES

Lourdes is a town in south-western France.

In 1858, a 14-year-old girl, Bernadette Soubirous, had a series of visions between 11 February and 16 July. These visions of the Virgin Mary were at the Massabielle grotto on the left bank of the stream.

The visions began on 11 February when Bernadette, her sister and a friend were looking for wood in the meadows. Bernadette did not wish to cross the stream because it was so cold and she had chronic asthma. She heard a noise like a gust of wind but none of the trees were moving. Then she saw a young woman smiling at here from the grotto.

The third vision took place on the 18 February and the Virgin spoke for the first time. She told Bernadette that she did not need to write down what she would say and asked her, 'Would you do me the kindness of coming here for 15 days?' and then said, 'I do not promise to make you happy in this world but in the other.'

During the thirteenth Apparition the Virgin said: 'Go, tell the priests to come here in procession and build a chapel here.'

Then on 25 March 1858, during the sixteenth Apparition, Bernadette went to the Grotto and asked the Lady for her name. She asked three times. Finally, she received the answer: 'Que soy era Immaculada Conceptiou' (I am the Immaculate Conception).

In 1862 Pope Pius IX said that the visions were authentic and authorised the prayer to Mary as Our Lady of Lourdes.

In 1866 Bernadette joined the Sisters of Charity and in 1877 she became a nun. She was recognised as a Saint by the church in 1925.

The underground spring in the grotto is said to have healing powers and Lourdes is now a major pilgrimage centre. More than five million pilgrims visit Lourdes every year in the hope of a cure for themselves or someone close to them.

Although many people have recovered from illnesses after visiting Lourdes, the Roman Catholic Church investigates each claim very carefully and since the first 'official' cure on 1 March 1858, only 66 cases have been accepted by the Church as genuinely being miraculous.

The basilica built over the grotto in 1876 soon became too small for the number of worshippers and a new underground church which holds 20,000 people was built in 1958.

ICT FOR RESEARCH

Using the internet find out more about the cures which have taken place at Lourdes and the ways in which the Roman Catholic Church tries to establish whether they are miracles.

WALSINGHAM

The village of Little Walsingham is in Norfolk, England.

In the eleventh century, the Lord of the Manor was Richeldis de Faverches. He died, leaving his widow and a young son Geoffrey who went on the Crusades.

Lady Richeldis was very religious and devoted her life to caring for others. In 1061 CE she had a vision. In this vision she was taken by the Virgin Mary to see the house in Nazareth where she had received the announcement from the Angel Gabriel that she was to be the mother of Jesus.

The Virgin asked Lady Richeldis to build an exact copy of the house in Walsingham. She had this vision three times and then gave the materials for the house to be built. The builders had little success on the first day. That night Lady Richeldis prayed for help to complete the project. She was unable to sleep and went to the site. Here she heard singing and saw angels leaving the completed building which was now 200 feet away from the original site.

From this time Walsingham became known as England's Nazareth.

Geoffrey de Faverches left instructions in his will for a Priory to be built at Walsingham and this was run by Augustinian Canons.

The priory contained the wooden house of Mary and soon became a very important place of pilgrimage. It was visited by Henry III, Edward II, Edward III, Henry IV, Edward IV, Henry VII and Henry VIII.

The priory grew to be very rich and famous until it was destroyed in 1538 by Henry VIII at the time of the dissolution of the monasteries.

Bitter, bitter, O to behold
The grass to grow
Where the walls of Walsingham
So stately did show

'The wrecks of Walsingham', Anon.

In 1897 Roman Catholic pilgrimage to Walsingham was restored. Just outside of the village is a fourteenth century building known as the Slipper Chapel – the Chapel of St Catherine. It was originally a resting place for people walking to the shrine. From here people walked barefoot to the Holy House. This building became the Roman Catholic National Shrine and contains a statue of Our Lady of Walsingham based on the image on the seal of the Priory.

In 1922, the Anglican Vicar of Walsingham, Father Hope Patten, placed a similar statue in the parish church of St Mary. Soon people again began to make pilgrimages to Walsingham. Then, in 1931, because of the very large number of pilgrims visiting Walsingham, a Pilgrim Hospice was opened and a new Holy House was built inside a small pilgrimage church. The church was enlarged in 1938 to provide more space for pilgrims.

The shrine has a Holy Well where pilgrims are sprinkled and from where people take home Holy Water for the sick.

The Russian Orthodox Church has three places of worship at Walsingham: Church of the Holy Transfiguration (in Great Walsingham), the Chapel of Saint Seraphim and the Chapel of the Life-Giving Spring of the Mother of God which is inside the Anglican Shrine.

COVENTRY

Coventry is a city in the West Midlands, England. In the Middle Ages it was famous for its cycle of Mystery Plays. These plays, which told stories, mainly from the Bible, were performed outdoors on carts which were pulled though the streets so that people in different parts of the town all had the opportunity to see them. The plays were usually performed on Saints' Days and festivals, especially Corpus Christi.

Coventry suffered great damage from bombing during the Second World War (1939–45) and only the spires of St Michael's Cathedral were left standing.

The Cathedral was rebuilt in 1962 by Sir Basil Spence. The modern design links to the bombed remains of the old building.

Of particular importance is the Chapel of Reconciliation in the new cathedral and many people go there as a pilgrimage to pray for peace.

CANTERBURY

Canterbury is a town in Kent in south-eastern England.

In 597 CE St Augustine landed on the Isle of Thanet. The King of Kent, Aethelberht I, was married to a Christian, Bertha, and she persuaded him to support Augustine's mission. Augustine was given the Queen's parish church, St Martin's. Augustine was consecrated at Arles as Bishop of the English and returned to Canterbury where he founded the Abbeys of SS. Peter and Paul, later known as St. Augustine's Abbey, and also built the cathedral, which was then called Christ Church.

In 1170 the Archbishop of Canterbury, Thomas à Becket, was murdered at the altar of the cathedral on the orders of King Henry II for refusing to obey him when Henry wanted to change the law about the punishment of priests who had committed crimes. In 1174 Henry went to the cathedral to seek forgiveness, and from that time onwards Becket's shrine became a centre for pilgrims from all over England. The cathedral was built between the eleventh and twelfth centuries and from the fourteenth to the sixteenth centuries.

The poet Geoffrey Chaucer (c.1342/43–1400) wrote a set of poems called the Canterbury Tales which are about a group of pilgrims making a pilgrimage to Canterbury to visit the Shrine of Thomas Becket.

Canterbury Cathedral.

The poems, many of which are very funny and rude, are written in Middle English, the language spoken in the fourteenth century. Here are the opening lines:

Whan that Aprill with his shoures soote
The droghte of March hath perced to the rrote,
And bathed every veyne in swich licour
Of which vertu engendered is the flour . . .

And here is a modern translation:
When in April the sweet showers fall
And pierce the drought of March to the root, and all
The veins are bathed in liquor of such power
As brings about the engendering of the flower,
When also Zephyrus with his sweet breath
Exhales an air in every grove and heath
Upon the tender shoots, and the young sun
His half-course in the sign of the Ram has run,
And the small fowl are making melody
That sleep away the night with open eye
(So nature pricks them and their heart engages)
Then people long to go on pilgrimages
And palmers long to seek the stranger strands
Of far-off saints, hallowed in sundry lands,
And specially, from every shire's end
In England, down to Canterbury they wend
To seek the holy blissful martyr, quick
To give his help to them when they were sick.
(tr. Nevil Coghill)

The Archbishop of Canterbury is now the primate of all England and so the senior bishop in the Anglican church.

ICT FOR RESEARCH

In a library find out about the different pilgrims who appear in The Canterbury Tales.

Also find out why King Henry II argued with Thomas a Becket.

COMPOSTELA

Santiago de Compostela is the capital of Galicia in north-western Spain.

In 813 CE a tomb was found near by at Padrón and the person who discovered it had a vision that it was the tomb of the apostle James who had been put to death in Jerusalem in 44 CE. His bones had apparently been taken to Spain because, according to the legend, he had preached there and converted the people to Christianity.

A church was built over the tomb and by the Middle Ages it was the most important place for Christian pilgrims after Rome and Jerusalem.

The town was destroyed in 997 CE but the tomb survived. The present cathedral was built in 1078.

St Francis is said to have visited Santiago in 1214 on a pilgrimage.

There is a series of roads running through France and Spain known as the Route of Santiago de Compostela. These are the routes travelled by pilgrims in the Middle Ages. After making the pilgrimage they wore a scallop shell on their clothing. The shell is the symbol of St James.

ICT FOR RESEARCH

Using Encarta or the internet find out who St James was and the role which he plays in the New Testament.

There are many different reasons for going on a pilgrimage. For some people it forms part of a holiday in a different country but as this chapter shows pilgrimage has always played an important part in Christian life.

Some people say that after making a pilgrimage they feel that their faith has been strengthened and they are more able to continue with their daily life. This may be because of something which happened to them spiritually when they visited a particular place or simply because it strengthens their faith to be somewhere where an important person within their religion once lived or taught.

PRACTICE EXAMINATION QUESTIONS

1 (a) **Describe a visit to a Christian place of pilgrimage. (8 marks)**

You need to identify the place of pilgrimage you are going to write about. You then need to describe it saying why it is a place of pilgrimage. For example, you might say what happened there or if someone important visited the place or is buried there.

(b) **Explain why some Christians go on pilgrimage and the effect that this might have on them. (7 marks)**

In this part of the question you need to explore some of the different reasons why people go on a pilgrimage. You then need to consider the possible effects which this might have on them afterwards. Some people may be healed or have their faith strengthened for example.

(c) **'There are more important things for Christians to do than to go on pilgrimage.'**
Do you agree? Give reasons to support your answer and show that you have thought about different points of view. You must refer to Christianity in your answer. (5 marks)

It is important to remember that you have to give different opinions in your answer to this question. You might want to argue that for some people, pilgrimage is the most important thing they could do whilst for others going to church regularly or working for a charity is more important. Remember to give reasons for your opinion.

2 (a) **Choose a place of Christian pilgrimage and describe what a pilgrim may do on a visit to this place. (8 marks)**

Once you have chosen a place of pilgrimage you need to describe fully what a pilgrim might do there. For example, if the place was Jerusalem you would need to detail some of the different parts of the city a pilgrim would want to visit and why.

(b) **Explain why pilgrimage may be important for the life and beliefs of a Christian today. (7 marks)**

In this part you need to say how a pilgrimage might strengthen the beliefs of a Christian and so perhaps make life easier for them. A pilgrimage might do this because they will probably meet other pilgrims, because they visit important places and know that they are standing in the place that, for example, Jesus and his disciples stood.

(c) **'Pilgrimages are just an excuse for a holiday.'**
Do you agree? Give reasons to support your answer and show that you have thought about different points of view. You must refer to Christianity in your answer. (5 marks)

You need to give different points of view in this section. You might think that the statement is certainly not true and you can say so but you have to explain why this is the case. You might also say, for example, that the benefits of going on a pilgrimage can be very similar to going on a holiday because you come home feeling rested and more able to cope with daily life.

3 (a) **Describe one place of pilgrimage in the Holy Land. (8 marks)**

In this question you are being asked to write specifically about one place in the Holy Land. Make sure that you choose one where there is enough to write about for your answer. For example, although Galilee is an important place in the life of Jesus, there is not very much that you can write in describing it. On the other hand, if you chose Jerusalem you would have a great deal to write about.

(b) **Explain why visiting the Holy Land might be very important to some Christians. (7 marks)**

Many Christians do feel that it is important to visit the Holy Land. They may want to see the places where Jesus lived and worked, where he was born and was crucified. They may also want to see the site of the Temple where he prayed. Many people say that visiting the Holy Land makes their faith much stronger as they can then visualise what it was like at the time when Jesus was teaching.

(c) 'You don't need to go on a journey to be close to God.'

Do you agree? Give reasons to support your answer and show that you have thought about different points of view. You must refer to Christianity in your answer. (*5 marks*)

Many people would say that this statement is true and that as God is everywhere then it does not matter where you are. Others might say that although the statement is true, it is much easier to worship God and feel closer to God in some places than in others so going on a pilgrimage might help people to feel closer to God.

4 (a) Describe two places of Christian pilgrimage. (*8 marks*)

You may choose any two places of pilgrimage. They may be similar or they may be very different from each other. They may be two places in the Holy Land or they may be the Holy Land in general and another place such as Lourdes. Look ahead to the rest of the question to anticipate how part (a) might link to part (b) and (c).

(b) Explain how and why places such as the two you have described became centres of Christian pilgrimage. (*7 marks*)

Look back at the first part of the question and decide how much more is needed to make it clear how and why the two places became centres of pilgrimage. Then consider if what you have written can help you make some general points about places of pilgrimage. Are the two places similar or different from each other and are either or both of them typical in some way of all places of pilgrimage?

(c) 'Pilgrimage is a selfish waste of time and money.'

Do you agree? Give reasons to support your answer and show that you have thought about different points of view. You must refer to Christianity in your answer. (*5 marks*)

Now you are concentrating on discussing the reasons why people might go on pilgrimage. You can draw on what you have written already to give examples to support the points you are making. You may wish to consider time and money separately. Remember to consider other points of view and how you might respond to them.

5

PLACES AND FORMS OF WORSHIP

PLACES OF WORSHIP

If most people were asked where Christians worshipped they would probably answer that it was in a church. However, there are many different names and buildings in which Christians worship together. Some of the names given to these are church, chapel, meeting house, citadel, cathedral, minster, abbey, monastery and priory.

THINKING POINT

Find out some of the main differences between these buildings and write a short explanation for the use of each name.

However, whatever name is given to this place of worship, they all serve the same purpose, which is to provide a place where Christians come together to worship:

For where two or three come together in my name, there am I with them.

(Matthew 18:20)

Most traditional churches are designed in the shape of a cross. Originally, they were probably a simple rectangle, based on a normal building. The earliest were converted houses called titulae.

The two main types of building found today are the basilica style which is a long building with a door at one end and an altar at the other, and a shape with a dome at the centre of a circular or polygon-shaped building.

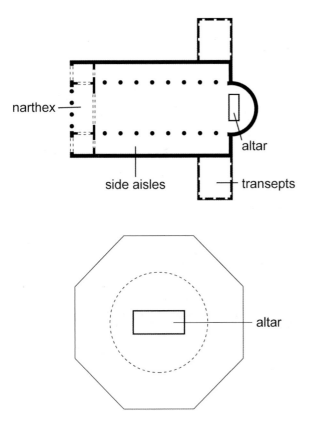

Many churches also have transepts – extra space at right angles to the main part of the building. These can be shorter than the main building to form a traditional Latin cross shape or can make all the parts of equal length as in a Greek cross.

Traditionally churches face east, towards Jerusalem. This means that the altar, where the Eucharist is celebrated, is placed at the east end of the church. The altar itself stands in a part of the church called the sanctuary and is usually separated from the rest of the church by a rail called the communion rail.

The part of the church which leads back from the chancel to the transepts, where a choir may sit, is the chancel. In some medieval churches the chancel is slightly angled towards the left. These are often called 'weeping chancels' and are said to represent the position of Jesus' head when he was on the cross.

At the entrance to the chancel there is sometimes a screen. This is known as a rood screen from an Old English word which meant 'cross' because many of these screens originally had a statue of Jesus on the cross fixed to the top of the screen.

The largest part of the church, where the congregation sit, is called the nave. This name is thought to come from the Latin word 'navis' meaning ship.

Often the main door will be at the far west end of the church and in this area is the baptistery. This is used for baptisms and contains the font. The font contains water for baptism and is placed at the west end of the church so that when children, or adults, come to be baptised, they ceremony takes place right at the entrance and they are then welcomed into the church.

These are the basic details of a church building but there is a very large variation in shapes and design across the world.

The outside of a church may be very simple or very elaborate depending on the style of the time in which it was built. Some churches have towers or steeples. These contain the church bells which have always been rung to warn people that a service was about to begin and also at times of celebration, such as festivals and marriages, and at times of mourning, such as funerals.

A church might simply be beside a busy street in a town or city, or it might stand in a graveyard in the country.

THINKING POINT

Look at some of the different styles of church buildings and try to find out what they are called and when they were built.

As well as the main features of a church building, there are many other furnishings inside which can play an important part in worship.

Many churches, particularly older ones, have stained glass windows. Although these may sometimes just be decorative, they were originally designed to tell stories from the Bible and from the lives of Christian saints. In the Middle Ages most people could not read and so these provided a way of reminding them of stories and teachings. At this time, the inside walls of churches were also used for paintings. In particular, the arch over the rood screen often contained very vivid paintings of the Day of Judgement and showed people being thrown into Hell.

The nave usually has pews, wooden benches with backs, for people to sit on, though some have wooden chairs.

Somewhere in the church, often in the chancel, there is usually an organ to provide music for services.

On the walls of the church there may be banners, pictures, or monuments to members of the church who have died.

Towards the front of the nave is the usual place for the pulpit. This word originally meant 'platform'. It is a raised place where the priest or minister stands to preach the sermon. Pulpits usually have a flight of steps so that the person preaching is raised above the nave and everyone can see and hear them.

Often placed opposite the pulpit is a lectern, a special stand on which the Bible is placed and from where it is read.

For many hundreds of years, it has been traditional for the altar to be placed at the far east end of the church. When the priest stood at the altar he then had his back to the people, 'facing God'. More recently some churches have moved the altar away from the east wall so that the priest is facing the people.

The altar may be of stone or wood and is usually covered with a coloured cloth which shows the season in the church's year (see page 35) and then a linen cloth on top.

The altar may have large candlesticks on it, usually two or six, which are lit during services. In the past these always served a practical purpose of providing light but are also a reminder that Jesus was the 'Light of the World'.

When Jesus spoke again to the people, he said, 'I am the light of the world. Whoever follows me will never walk in darkness, but will have the light of life.' (John 8:12)

In the wall behind the altar or to the side is often a box called a tabernacle. Here the consecrated bread is placed after the Eucharist. It can then be taken by the priest to anyone who is too sick to attend church. Sometimes this tabernacle hangs over the altar and is then called a pyx. Near the tabernacle there will be a light burning to show that the consecrated bread is inside.

A church may have several altars and there are often others placed in the transepts. When this happens the main altar in the east is called the High Altar.

Every church is dedicated to a particular biblical person or saint and the side altars may then be named for other saints or sometimes events in the life of Jesus. Sometimes these altars may have statues or pictures of these saints above them.

Some churches, particularly Roman Catholic ones, have statues of the Saints around the church and people light votive candles and place them in front of the statues, asking the particular saint to pray for them. There will also be crosses and crucifixes. A crucifix is a cross with the image of Jesus on it.

Around the walls of the church may be pictures of the 14 Stations of the Cross.

When the Franciscans were given custody of the holy places in Jerusalem in the 1300s they developed these 14 Stations of the Cross so that pilgrims could pray along the Via Dolorosa (see page 42) following in the steps of Jesus.

Each station represents an event in the last day of Jesus' life. Seven of the events come from the gospels and the others are traditional.

These are the 14 stations, followed by the traditional Franciscan prayers said at each one:

1   Jesus is condemned by Pilate (Matthew 27:15–26)
    O Jesus! so meek and uncomplaining, teach me resignation in trials.
2   Jesus receives the cross (John 19:17)
    My Jesus, this Cross should be mine, not Thine; my sins crucified Thee.
3   Jesus falls under the weight of the cross
    O Jesus! by this first fall, never let me fall into mortal sin.
4   Jesus meets Mary
    O Jesus! may no human tie, however dear, keep me from following the road of the Cross.
5   Simon of Cyrene carries the Cross for Jesus (Matthew 27:32)
    Simon unwillingly assisted Thee; may I with patience suffer all for Thee.
6   Saint Veronica wipes Jesus' face
    O Jesus! Thou didst imprint Thy sacred features upon Veronica's veil; stamp them also indelibly upon my heart.
7   Jesus falls again
    By Thy second fall, preserve me, dear Lord, from relapse into sin.
8   Jesus speaks to the women of Jerusalem (Luke 23:27–31)
    My greatest consolation would be to hear Thee say: 'Many sins are forgiven thee, because thou hast loved much.'
9   Jesus falls for a third time
    O Jesus! when weary upon life's long journey, be Thou my strength and my perseverance.

10 Jesus' clothes are removed (Matthew 27:28)
    My soul has been robbed of its robe of innocence;
    clothe me, dear Jesus, with the garb of penance
    and contrition.

11 The crucifixion
    Thou didst forgive Thy enemies; my God, teach
    me to forgive injuries and FORGET *them.*

12 Jesus dies (Matthew 27:45–56)
    Thou art dying, my Jesus, but Thy Sacred Heart
    still throbs with love for Thy sinful children.

13 Mary receives Jesus' body
    Receive me into thy arms, O Sorrowful Mother;
    and obtain for me perfect contrition for my sins.

14 Jesus is buried (Matthew 27:57–61)
    When I receive Thee into my heart in Holy
    Communion, O Jesus, make it a fit abiding place
    for thy adorable Body. Amen.

Particularly during Lent, people may walk from one station to the next, stopping and praying at each one.

Many Protestant churches may be much plainer than this. The Protestant churches tend not to have statues or images in them. In the Ten Commandments it says:

> You shall not make for yourself an idol in the form of anything in heaven above or on the earth beneath or in the waters below. You shall not bow down to them or worship them; for I, the LORD your God, am a jealous God, punishing the children for the sin of the fathers to the third and fourth generation of those who hate me, but showing love to a thousand generations of those who love me and keep my commandments.
>
> (Exodus 20:4–6)

Protestants believe that having statues in a church would break this Commandment.

Protestant churches have an altar and font but the altar may not be given the same central importance as it is in a Roman Catholic church. Instead the pulpit may be central to the building. In some chapels the pulpit is placed on the centre of the east wall above the altar. This shows the importance

which they give to the Ministry of the Word – the preaching of the Bible.

In a Baptist church there is a large tank under the floor at the front of the church. When an adult is ready to be baptised this is uncovered so that they can receive baptism by total immersion under the water.

Eastern Orthodox Churches are also of a different design.

At the west end is the narthex. This may contain pictures of the Last Judgement and of scenes from the Old Testament. The font is placed in the narthex.

In the nave there are very few seats, just ones for the old or sick. People stand during services.

At the front of the nave is the iconostasis. This is a screen covered in icons (pictures) of the saints. In the centre of the iconostasis are the Royal Doors which are opened during certain parts of the Liturgy. In front of the Doors is a small platform called the Amvon on which the priest stands.

Behind the doors, the whole area of the sanctuary is called the altar. It contains the Holy Table where the Liturgy is celebrated.

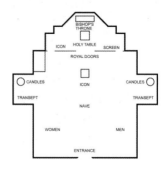

The simplest of all Christian places of worship is a Meeting House. These buildings are used by Quakers – the Religious Society of Friends. They consist of nothing more than a very plain room without any decoration, with rows of chairs and a table. During worship Quakers sit in silence and wait for one of their members to be moved to speak.

Christian places of worship vary enormously and it is not possible to say that every place of worship has at least one common factor. The buildings and their design and furnishings have developed over hundreds of years to suit the needs of the worshippers who use them. Many people find elaborate churches and statues helpful to concentrate their thoughts while they are worshipping, whilst others find this a distraction and prefer a simple space where they can sit and think and pray.

Whatever the design, however, all Christian places of worship are designed to praise God and to provide a place where Christians can come together and worship.

Of course, as well as being used for worship on Sundays and other days, many churches and church buildings provide community centres for the local congregation. Different groups of people may arrange meetings there to discuss church business or other aspects of community life, and fund-raising and social functions are often held in church halls. So, the church can be seen as standing at the centre of the local Christian community as well as being the place for worship.

TYPES OF WORSHIP

The type of services which take place in a church may vary between the different denominations to whom a particular building belongs.

The most common service of all is probably the Eucharist – from a Greek word meaning 'giving thanks'. This is often called by other names such as Holy Communion, Mass, Lord's Supper, Breaking of Bread and Liturgy.

However, the event with which it is concerned is the same.

> *The Lord Jesus, on the night he was betrayed, took bread, and when he had given thanks, he broke it and said, 'This is my body, which is for you; do this in remembrance of me.' In the same way, after supper he took the cup, saying, 'This cup is the new covenant in my blood; do this, whenever you drink it, in remembrance of me.'* (1 Corinthians 11:23b–25)

This took place at the Last Supper which Jesus ate with his disciples before he was crucified. He shared bread and wine with them and said that this made a new covenant to replace the covenants which God had previously made with the Jews.

This account by Paul in 1 Corinthians is the earliest we have. There are also accounts in the gospels.

LOOK UP

Look up the gospel accounts of the Last Supper in Matthew 26:26–28, Mark 14:22–24 and Luke 22:17–20 and compare them.

The Eucharist has become central to Christian worship and many denominations have services in which the priest or minister repeats the words of Jesus before bread and wine are distributed among the congregation.

However, people have different beliefs about what happens at the Eucharist.

The Roman Catholic Church teaches a doctrine called Transubstantiation. This says that when the priest blesses the bread and wine using Jesus' words, although the bread and wine still look the same, they have become the actual body and blood of Jesus. Jesus has died again so that Christians can be free from sin. When the worshippers receive the bread and wine they are actually receiving Jesus into their bodies.

Incense is used in many services to show the prayers of the faithful rising up to God

In the sixteenth century, the Protestant reformers (see pages 68–9) came to believe in Consubstantiation. This says that the bread and wine remain bread and wine but are also the body and blood of Jesus.

More recently some people have come to believe in receptionism. This teaches that the bread and wine become the body and blood of Jesus when they are received by a Christian.

Finally, some Christians reject the whole of this teaching. They believe instead in memorialism. This means that the Eucharist is simply a memorial of what Jesus did. They are following his teachings and instructions to 'do this in remembrance of me'.

For many Christians, the celebration of the Eucharist and receiving Holy Communion is at the centre of their worship. In the Roman Catholic Church and some Anglican Churches the Eucharist or mass is celebrated every day. For some other Christians this may be a weekly or monthly event.

As well as the Eucharist many Christians attend other services of worship. This usually consists of prayers, bible readings, hymns and a sermon. These services stress the Ministry of the Word and the importance of hearing the teachings of the Bible and of worshipping and praying to God. These services may be very formal ones or, especially in evangelical churches, they may be very interactive with lots of singing and music and also, in many cases, people speaking in tongues.

The idea of glossolalia or speaking in tongues is found in the Acts of the Apostles.

When the day of Pentecost came, they were all together in one place. Suddenly a sound like the blowing of a violent wind came from heaven and filled the whole house where they were sitting. They saw what seemed to be tongues of fire that separated and came to rest on each of them. All of them were filled with the Holy Spirit and began to speak in other tongues as the Spirit enabled them.

Now there were staying in Jerusalem God-fearing Jews from every nation under heaven. When they heard this sound, a crowd came together in bewilderment, because each one heard them speaking in his own language. Utterly amazed, they asked: 'Are not all these men who are speaking Galileans? Then how is it that each of us hears them in his own native language? Parthians,

Medes and Elamites; residents of Mesopotamia, Judea and Cappadocia, Pontus and Asia, Phrygia and Pamphylia, Egypt and the parts of Libya near Cyrene; visitors from Rome (both Jews and converts to Judaism); Cretans and Arabs – we hear them declaring the wonders of God in our own tongues!' (Acts 2:1–11)

From this time onwards, many Christians have found themselves so moved by their worshipping, that they have been able to speak in tongues in languages which they cannot understand themselves.

Many Christians may also worship on their own in private or with their family at home. They may choose readings from the Bible and then pray to worship God.

Prayer is a very important aspect of Christian life and worship. As well as there being many different prayers there are different types of prayer. Some are formal set prayers such as the Our Father and the prayers which are said during services in church. Some prayers are spontaneous when a person just wants to speak to God at a particular moment.

When some people pray they may use petitionary prayer, this could be asking God to intervene in the world. Sometimes people may pray for another person who is ill – this is intercessory prayer.

Many prayers are said just to thank God for what has happened or for life and existence in general.

Sometimes Christians may meditate, they sit quietly and try to empty their minds of ordinary thought and listen to their spiritual feelings.

One of the commonest forms of prayer, particularly in the Roman Catholic Church, is the use of the Rosary.

The rosary is said to have been developed by St Dominic in the thirteenth century. It consists of a string of beads with a crucifix hanging from them. The beads are divided into five sets of one large bead and ten smaller ones. Each set is called a decade.

At the beginning of saying the rosary, the worshipper blesses themselves with the crucifix and then says the Apostles' Creed (see page 8), the Our Father (see page 26), three Hail Marys

> Hail, Mary, full of grace
> the Lord is with thee;
> Blessed art thou among women,
> And blessed is thy fruit of thy womb, Jesus.
> Holy Mary, Mother of God
> Pray for us sinners,
> Now and at the hour of our death.
> Amen

and the Glory be

> Glory be to the Father
> And to the Son
> And to the Holy Spirit;
> As it was in the beginning
> Is now, and ever shall be
> World without end.
> Amen

Then, meditating on one of the sets of five mysteries, the worshipper says one Our Father and ten Hail Marys and one Glory be ... for each decade. At the end of saying the rosary the prayer Hail Holy Queen is said.

> Hail, Holy Queen.
> Mother of Mercy,
> Our life, our sweetness,
> And our hope
> To you do we cry,
> Poor banished children of Eve.
> To you do we send up our sighs,
> Mourning and weeping
> In this valley of tears.
> Turn, then, Most Gracious advocate,
> Your eyes of mercy towards us,
> And after this, our exile,
> Show unto us
> The blessed fruit of your womb, Jesus.

O clement, O loving, O sweet Virgin Mary.
Pray for us, O Holy Mother of God.
That we may be made worthy of
The promises of Christ.
Amen

There are three sets of Mysteries:

The Joyful Mysteries

1 The Annunciation – Luke 1:26–38
2 The Visitation – Luke 1:39–45
3 The Nativity – Luke 2:6–19
4 The Presentation in the Temple – Luke 2: 22–40
5 The Finding in the Temple – Luke 2: 41–52

The Sorrowful Mysteries

1 The Agony in the Garden – Luke 22: 39–53
2 The Scourging at the Pillar – John 19:1
3 The Crowning with Thorns – John 19: 2–3
4 Carrying the Cross – Luke 23:26–32
5 The Crucifixion – Luke 23: 33–46

The Glorious Mysteries

1 The Resurrection – Luke 24: 1–8
2 The Ascension – Acts 1: 6–12
3 The Descent of the Holy Spirit – Acts 2: 1–4
4 The Assumption of the Virgin – Psalms 45:10, 14, 15
5 The Coronation of the Virgin – Revelation 12:1–2, 5

ICT FOR RESEARCH

Look at the bible references for the mysteries. You will see that the last two mysteries do not appear in the New Testament. Find out something about these two and try to explain why these texts might have been chosen for them.

LEADERS OF WORSHIP

Just as there are many different names for Christian places of worship there are also different names given to people or ministers who lead the worship in these communities.

In the Roman Catholic Church the Pope, the Bishop of Rome, is the leader of the church.

Pope John XXIII

A three tier papal tiara

In Matthew's gospel, the following passage appears:

> When Jesus came to the region of Caesarea Philippi, he asked his disciples, 'Who do people say the Son of Man is?' They replied, 'Some say John the Baptist; others say Elijah; and still others, Jeremiah or one of the prophets.' 'But what about you?' he asked. 'Who do you say I am?' Simon Peter answered, 'You are the Christ, the Son of the living God.'
> Jesus replied, 'Blessed are you, Simon son of Jonah, for this was not revealed to you by man, but by my Father in heaven. And I tell you that you are Peter, and on this rock I will build my church, and the gates of Hades will not overcome it. I will give you the keys of the kingdom of heaven.'
> (Matthew 16:13–19a)

This passage is often called the Petrine Commission. The Roman Catholic Church teaches that St Peter founded the church in Rome and that he passed his authority on directly to the Bishop of Rome. Each Pope has passed on his authority, therefore, the Pope has a direct line of authority from Peter and so he is Head of the Christian Church.

The next order of ministers are called Bishops – from a Greek word meaning overseer. In the Roman Catholic Church the Bishops and Archbishops receive their authority from the Pope and oversee the work of priests in their diocese.

Priests are generally in charge of individual churches. Here they have to be like shepherds to their congregations, conducting services and counselling and teaching them. They are often called Parish Priests.

All these ministers have to be ordained priests by bishops and bishops by the Pope. This placing of hands on the person's head gives them the authority and power to be ministers and ensures the Apostolic Succession – the belief that this power has been passed in a direct line from St Peter.

Someone who has been ordained but is not yet a priest is called a deacon. Deacons were first appointed in the early church.

The first people we think of as deacons were appointed by the disciples.

LOOK UP

Look up the references to deacons in Acts 6, Philippians 1:1; 1 Timothy 3:8–13.

The name Presbyter which is sometimes used, was used in first century for an administrative official of a local church. Today it is most commonly used for a minister in a Protestant church, such as the Presbyterian church. In churches such as this the ministers are lay people – people who are not ordained but take part in services. They may read from the Bible, lead prayers and services, preach and carry out many other tasks within the local Christian community.

Some people choose to give up what we might think of as normal life and instead go to live in monasteries, away from the world. Details of these can be found in Chapter 6.

FOR DISCUSSION

There are many other names and titles used for Christian ministers such as Vicar, Rector, Chaplain, Curate, Dean, Archdeacon, Patriarch. Find out what these names mean and why they are used.

SACRAMENTAL WORSHIP

A sacrament is a way in which the grace and the power of God can be received.

St Augustine of Hippo said that a sacrament was an 'outward and visible sign of an inward and spiritual grace'.

According to Roman Catholic teaching once a sacrament is performed properly it gives the person God's grace regardless of the faith of the person who receives it. This is known as ex opera operato – from work already done.

The Protestant Church recognises only two sacraments, baptism and the Eucharist, as these are found in the New Testament and were brought into existence by Jesus. Therefore, these are often called the Dominical Sacraments (Dominical means 'from the Lord').

BAPTISM (see page 113)

Then Jesus came from Galilee to the Jordan to be baptised by John. (Matthew 5:13)

EUCHARIST (see pages 68–9)

While they were eating, Jesus took bread, gave thanks and broke it, and gave it to his disciples, saying, 'Take and eat; this is my body.'

Then he took the cup, gave thanks and offered it to them, saying, 'Drink from it, all of you. This is my blood of the covenant, which is poured out for many for the forgiveness of sins'.

(Matthew 26:26–28)

The Roman Catholic Church also recognises five other sacraments: confirmation (see pages 115–16), reconciliation or penance, anointing of the sick or extreme unction, Holy Orders, and marriage (see page 116).

RECONCILIATION

This is sometimes called the sacrament of penance or absolution.

When Jesus gave Peter the Petrine Commission he said:

> 'Whatever you bind on earth will be bound in heaven, and whatever you loose on earth will be loosed in heaven.' (Matthew 16:19b)

Jesus also repeats this after the resurrection:

> Again Jesus said, 'Peace be with you! As the Father has sent me, I am sending you.' And with that he breathed on them and said, 'Receive the Holy Spirit. If you forgive anyone his sins, they are forgiven; if you do not forgive them, they are not forgiven.' (John 20:21–23)

The Church has interpreted this to mean that priests have the power to forgive sins on behalf of God. Many Christians go to make their confession every week. They kneel in a small room called a confessional and, speaking to the priest through a grille or curtain they tell him what sins they have committed since their last confession. They acknowledge that they are truly sorry for these sins and will try not to commit them again. After this the priest will absolve them of their sins. They may then be asked to perform a penance such as saying a particular prayer or prayers.

> They went out and preached that people should repent. They drove out many demons and anointed many sick people with oil and healed them. (Mark 6:13)

> Is any one of you sick? He should call the elders of the church to pray over him and anoint him with oil in the name of the Lord. And the prayer offered in faith will make the sick person well; the Lord will raise him up. If he has sinned, he will be forgiven. Therefore confess your sins to each other and pray for each other so that you may be healed. The prayer of a righteous man is powerful and effective. (James 5:14–16)

ANOINTING OF THE SICK

In this ceremony, someone who is seriously ill or dying is blessed by the priest. After some bible readings and prayers, the priest anoints the person five times: on the eyes, ears, nose, lips and hands. The oil used is that which has been blessed by a bishop during a service on Maundy Thursday.

HOLY ORDERS

In Holy Orders or ordination a bishop lays his hands on the person who is to become a priest and in this way the sacrament is passed on. The priest now has the necessary spiritual power and authority to carry out his task.

Although the Anglican Church does not generally recognise ordination as a sacrament, it calls it a 'sacramental rite'.

PRACTICE EXAMINATION QUESTIONS

1 (a) Describe the main features of a Christian place of worship and its furnishings. (*8 marks*)

When answering this question you need to choose a place of worship that has enough to write about. You may choose a church or a chapel but probably a Quaker Meeting House would not really have enough to be said about it. You need to decide what main features you are going to write about, for example, altar, pulpit, font, and then say what they are used for.

(b) Explain the significance of these features and furnishings for the worshipper and how they reflect and assist belief. (*7 marks*)

In this section you need to think about how these features and furnishings are used during a service and the ways in which they can help someone in their worship and to focus their thoughts on God.

(c) 'You do not need to go to a place of public worship to be a Christian.'

Do you agree? Give reasons to support your answer and show that you have thought about different points of view. (*5 marks*)

Remember that in this section you do need to give different viewpoints. You may say that it is helpful for Christians to come together to worship and that some services such as the Eucharist need other people to be present. On the other hand, you might say that Christians can talk to God anywhere and at anytime.

2 (a) Describe a typical Eucharist service. (*8 marks*)

You need to choose a Eucharist service in a particular denomination and describe what takes place and why this is done.

(b) Explain the importance of attending a Eucharist for Christians. (*7 marks*)

Here you should explain that some people may attend a Eucharist daily whilst others go less often. You have the opportunity to explain that people are coming into the presence of Christ by taking part in the Eucharist and what this may mean to them.

(c) 'Modern Eucharist services fulfil Jesus' command to "do this in remembrance of me".'

Do you agree? Give reasons to support your answer and show that you have thought about different points of view. (*5 marks*)

In answering this question you may want to show how the Eucharist fulfils Jesus' instruction but you may also say that the original celebration at the Last Supper was a very simple event and that the modern service is not very much like it.

3 (a) Describe how Christians pray both together and in private prayer. (*8 marks*)

Here you should describe different types of prayer such as formal and spontaneous prayer and also those such as petitionary and intercessory. You could also write about the use of items such as the rosary or looking at a lighted candle or a picture while praying.

(b) Explain how regular prayer might affect the life and attitudes of a Christian believer. (*7 marks*)

In this question you need to think about the way in which praying regularly might help people feel closer to God and might also make them feel more able to carry out the tasks of their daily lives.

(c) 'Christian parents should teach their children to pray and young people should be asked to take part in Christian prayers at school.'

Do you agree? Give reasons to support your answer and show that you have thought about different points of view. (*5 marks*)

When you answer a question like this you need to think about the consequences of different viewpoints. You could say that it is the duty of Christian parents to bring their children up in this way to ensure that they lead a life following God's teachings. On the other hand you might say that children should be left to make up their own minds and not be forced into doing something like this until they can decide for themselves about their religion.

6

RELIGION IN THE COMMUNITY AND THE FAMILY

For where two or three come together in my name, there am I with them.

(Matthew 18:20)

Christianity has always had a sense of community, from small Christian groups huddled together at the beginning in times of persecution to the large worldwide Church and the community of saints which spans all history past, present and future.

The idea of a special community is an important theme in the Bible.

From ancient times, the Jews have seen themselves as a sacred community. They see themselves as a covenant people. They have a special relationship with God and with each other. They are one big family and their individual family units are each a microcosm. Each family is a mirror that shows the whole of Judaism.

The Jewish Scriptures tell of a series of covenants God made. Some were with individual people such as Adam and Noah and were significant for the whole human race.

Others were made by God with the Jewish nation through holy men such as Abraham and Moses. Abraham is often said to have been the patriarchal father of the people and Moses was the lawgiver who created the political nation. The kings and the chosen people all had a great responsibility. They had to live by God's law as a witness to the rest of the world. Jews today continue to live according to the Jewish law and to stress the importance of community and family.

In Christian teaching, the New Testament continues the theme of the Covenant that was written about in the Jewish Scriptures. Most Christians believe the New Covenant supersedes the Old Covenant. That means it does not destroy the past but it builds upon and develops the key ideas.

It is important in any study of Christianity to remember that Jesus of Nazareth was Jewish.

Christians place great importance on a prophecy which Jesus referred to at the Last Supper. The prophecy was made by the prophet Jeremiah in the seventh century BCE.

> 'The time is coming,' declares the Lord, 'when I will make a new covenant with the house of Israel and with the house of Judah. It will not be like the covenant I made with their forefathers when I took them by the hand to lead them out of Egypt, because they broke my covenant, though I was a husband to them,' declares the Lord.
>
> 'This is the covenant that I will make with the house of Israel after that time,' declares the Lord. 'I will put my law in their minds and write it on their hearts. I will be their God, and they will be my people. No longer will a man teach his neighbour, or a man his brother, saying, "Know the Lord," because they will all know me, from the least of them to the greatest,' declares the Lord. 'For I will forgive their wickedness and will remember their sins no more.'　　　(Jeremiah 31:31–34)

Jesus said: 'This is the New Covenant in my blood'. (Luke 22:20)

Christians believe that everyone who follows Jesus can become part of the covenant people.

THE WORK OF RELIGIOUS COMMUNITIES

Jesus taught that the two greatest principles to follow in life were love God and love your neighbour. The early Church in Jerusalem is portrayed in the New Testament as a caring community full of ideals about equality and sharing. Throughout history, Christians have been inspired by this example to try to implement the teaching of Jesus in practical ways.

> They devoted themselves to the apostles' teaching and to the fellowship, to the breaking of bread and to prayer. Everyone was filled with awe, and many wonders and miraculous signs were done by the apostles. All the believers were together and had everything in common. Selling their possessions and goods, they gave to anyone as he had need. Every day they continued to meet together in the temple courts. They broke bread in their homes and ate together with glad and sincere hearts, praising God and enjoying the favour of all the people. And the Lord added to their number daily those who were being saved.　　　(Acts 2:42–47)

Seven deacons, including Stephen, the first Christian martyr, and Philip were originally appointed to supervise the distribution of food to widows in the Christian community in Jerusalem.

The only criterion to be a deacon seems to have been that the deacons were men of faith and full of the Holy Spirit. Most of the seven have Greek names and one was a proselyte, a Gentile who had been a convert to Judaism before becoming a Christian.

Christians, despite their differences about doctrine or practice, have always interpreted the Christian gospel in terms of justice and concern and care for others.

Some Christians feel called to form or join enclosed religious communities in order to pray, live and work in purity away from the world but they are still praying for God's will to be done in the world. They are seeking to love God and love their neighbour. They may join monasteries, convents or other communities. Christians believe that prayer is very powerful.

> Benedict was born in Nursia, Italy around the year 480 CE. He was a hermit at first but eventually he formed a religious community on Mounte Cassino, north of Naples. He had a monastery built and was the abbot until his death around 547 CE. Benedict made rules for his monks which had a great influence on monastic life in the western world. Today, some Christian men and women still follow Benedict's rules. They have a life which is balanced in that they have prayer, study and also manual work.

Benedict's Rule 16

This meant they prayed when they rose from bed, then at six and at nine in the morning, at noon, at 3 p.m., at evening prayers and before they went to bed.

LAUDS	praise	6am
PRIME	first hour	9am
TERCE	third hour	noon
NONE	ninth hour	3pm
VESPERS	evening	evening prayer
COMPLINE	complete	final night prayer

SOME ROMAN CATHOLIC RELIGIOUS ORDERS

- Benedictines started in the sixth century.
- Cistercian monks wore white robes. Sometimes called White monks, they were founded in 1098. They were named after the Latin name for their place of origin in Burgundy in France, near Dijon. They were very influential in the twelfth century and their communities had a great influence on farming methods in Europe. Many of the abbeys became very wealthy.
- Augustinians – also known as Austins – follow the rules of St Augustine of Hippo in North Africa who died in 430 CE. Some of the original followers of Augustine's teachings were hermits but they fled to Italy when North Africa was invaded. In the eleventh century many men and women joined the Augustinians and they became one of the great mendicant orders of the Middle Ages. Mendicant means begging. When monks and nuns in any religion take vows of poverty, they live a simple austere life and have to rely on other people to give them food. Like Augustine, Augustinians spend a lot of time studying the Bible and theology. The Protestant reformer Martin Luther was originally an Augustinian monk and priest.

- Carmelites – about 1155 some pilgrims and crusaders settled on Mount Carmel and tried to live like Elijah the prophet. They were hermits who lived in cells. Eventually they formed communities and spread. Teresa of Avila, a Carmelite nun (1515–1582) founded a convent in 1562 which set the rules that reformed Carmelite communities observe. Juan de Yepes (mystic and poet now known as St John of the Cross) applied the same principles for Carmelite monks. Teresa was made a saint in 1622. She was made a doctor of the church in 1970 by Pope Paul VI and was the first woman to be given this honour.

- Dominican friars started at the end of the twelfth century. Their founder was St Dominic. Friars are monks who travel around preaching and teaching. Dominican friars are sometimes called Black Friars because they wore black robes. Thomas Aquinas c.1224–1274 was a Dominican. He was a great theologian and had a large influence on the theology of the Roman Catholic Church.

- The Franciscan Order is the largest in the Roman Catholic Church. It was started by St Francis of Assisi in the thirteenth century and is made up of three main groups:
  - priests and lay brothers who swear to live a life of prayer, preaching and penance
  - the Order of St Clare – cloistered nuns known also as the Poor Clares
  - lay men and women, some of whom live in communities and others who live in the world without taking vows but have committed themselves to teach, do works of charity and social service as St Francis did.

ICT FOR RESEARCH

Find out about the life of St Francis from Encarta or an encyclopaedia such as Britannica.

- Franciscans wear brown robes but they used to wear grey so they were called Grey Friars. Franciscans have been active in foreign missions and in many areas of scholarly study. So far, 98 saints and six popes were Franciscans.
- The Jesuits are members of the Society of Jesus founded by St Ignatius Loyola (1491–1556) who had been a Spanish soldier. They see themselves as soldiers of Christ obedient to the Pope. They are known for their missionary and charitable works but especially for education and scholarship. Jesuits had a prominent role in the Counter Reformation. There was opposition to the political power of the Jesuits and they were disbanded from 1773 to 1814. Pope Pius VII re-established the Society, and today the Jesuits are the largest Order of male religious persons in the Church.
- Trappists were founded by Armand de Rancé (1626–1700) at the Cistercian Abbey of La Trappe in France. All religious orders tend to take vows of poverty, chastity and obedience but Trappists also observe absolute silence. They were the first religious order to revive in France after the French Revolution and have continued increasing their abbeys which are found worldwide.

Saint Augustine was Bishop of Hippo for 35 years but he had also been a teacher and professor in Carthage, Rome and Milan. Augustine was very conscious of his own failings and he stressed the Christian teaching of original sin. *The Confessions* tell of his conversion in his early thirties and his remorse for the way he lived as a young man.

His conversion experience came in a garden in Milan when he heard a child's voice saying, 'Take up and read.' There was a Bible near by and Augustine read from Paul's letters about forgiveness of sin and peace with God. It was a turning point in his life. A well-known quotation from Augustine is: 'Thou hast made us for Thyself, O Lord, and our hearts are restless until they rest in Thee.'

Another book, *The City of God*, took Augustine 13 years to write. It was his vision of the role of the Christian Church on earth. He lived at the time when the Roman Empire, then mostly a Christian Empire, was losing its power. Some Romans said it was because the empire had neglected the old Roman gods. The imminent fall of the Roman Empire also shook the faith of many Christians. They could not believe God would let it happen. Augustine wrote that the Church was not confined to one city or empire. The Church was the City of God that existed in the hearts of the Christians. That City could never fall.

There are monks and nuns in the Eastern Orthodox Churches too. As Christianity spread to different countries in the East, a monastic tradition developed in each area. There are no special Orders like the ones that developed in the West. In the Orthodox Church, monks live together under the rule of an archimandrite, a sort of abbot. Archimandrites are elected and each monastery, convent or hermitage has its own rules. Some monks, but not all, may also be ordained as priests. Some become bishops.

Many religious communities are not enclosed orders. They are very much involved in the world.

THE MISSIONARIES OF CHARITY

This order was started in Calcutta by Mother Teresa and has two branches in Bangalore which take care of the homeless, poor and dying of all castes and all religions.

Agnes Gonxha Bejaxhiu was born in Skopje, the capital of the Republic of Macedonia. She entered the order of the Sisters of Our Lady of Loreto at the age of 18 and took the name Teresa. She taught in the Order's school in Calcutta until 1946 when she received 'a call within a call' to aid the desperately

poor of India. She received permission from Rome to leave her convent and began her work by bringing dying persons from the streets into a home where they could die in peace and dignity. She also established an orphanage. Other women joined her and in 1950 she received official approval for a congregation of sisters, called the Missionaries of Charity, whose members are dedicated to serving the poorest of the poor. Mother Teresa was awarded the 1979 Nobel Peace Prize.

Though some Protestants such as Anglicans have some monks and nuns, and places of retreat, the majority of Protestants do not have religious orders. Some Protestants are suspicious of religious orders which have monks or nuns because:

- events in past history have left a lasting impression on some Protestants. At the time of the Protestant Reformation, in the sixteenth century in Europe, organised religion had become corrupt
- some denominations think religious orders are élitist and separatist. They feel it is important to emphasise the equality of believers, especially when democracy is part of their country's culture
- some believe that because Christianity has to be the salt of the earth and the light shining in the world (Matthew 5) that the Christians have to be living fully in the real world to do this.

The majority of Christian denominations have groups of believers who do charitable works such as helping the sick, teaching, working with the poor, the homeless, refugees and the victims of natural disasters, earthquakes, floods and famines. Short-term emergency aid is given, such as water, food, blankets, medical aid, drainage and sanitation. The long-term aim is to help people to become independent and self-sufficient and able to help others.

It has been said that religion, including Christianity, is the curse of the world. It is true that Christians have condoned slavery and other injustices but it is also true that individual Christians have listened to their conscience and played a large part in social reform. The Quaker Elizabeth Fry, 1780–1845, campaigned for prison reform. People like John Woolman (1720–72), Granville Sharp (1735–1813) and William Wilberforce (1759–1833) campaigned against slavery. The Slavery Abolition Act was passed one month after the death of Wilberforce.

Many Christians support communities which campaign for peace and reconciliation such as Taizé, Corrymeela and the Community of the Cross of Nails. They petition governments and try to stop the exploitation of the developing countries by the richer more powerful countries and to identify the other factors which cause war and suffering and damage to the environment.

FOR DISCUSSION

Some Christians have felt in the past and in the present that Christians can best show their witness by keeping away from the corruption of secular life.

Sometimes they do this as whole communities or as families or as individuals.

- How far do you think Christians could and should keep away from secular modern life?
- Is there – or should there be – any connection between religion and politics?
- Some people think that Christian charities only help people so that they can preach the gospel to them. To what extent do you think this is a fair comment?

Monks and monasteries had a large part to play in the spread of Christianity. In the British Isles a flourishing Celtic Church already existed when Italian monks, sent by Pope Gregory I in Rome, arrived on the Isle of Thanet in the south of England in 597 CE. Irish monks, for example, Columbanus and Gallus had travelled through Europe and Ninian to Scotland. Brendan is said to have gone to the land which became America and, about 563 CE, Columba had sailed with twelve companions to the island of Iona off the west coast of Scotland.

In 635 CE Aidan went from Iona to found a monastery on Lindisfarne. His work was continued by Cuthbert who died in 687 CE on the island of Farne and is buried in Durham Cathedral.

There were Christian women in religious communities also. For example, Hilda, the Abbess of Whitby in Northumbria, presided over the Synod of Whitby 663/664 CE when it was decided that Britain would follow the Roman form of Christianity.

Monasteries have produced great scholars such as the Venerable Bede (672/3–735 CE), theologian and historian. He was buried at Jarrow in the north-east of England where he was born but his remains are now in Durham Cathedral.

Some of the ideas that recognise the role Christianity might play in the future have come from Christians who were part of religious communities:

TEILHARD DE CHARDIN (1881–1955)

He was a Jesuit, philosopher and paleontologist, and was famous for his religious theories of evolution. He argued that when humankind appeared on the earth an added dimension was brought to the world's development. It was the start of rational reflection. He is quoted as saying that animals know but humans *know* that they know. He believed that the evolution of humans is part of God's plan and, eventually, socialization of the whole human race will lead to the cosmic redemption of the universe.

THOMAS MERTON (1915–1968)

A Roman Catholic, Trappist monk, American poet, writer and priest whose early education was in England and France. He encouraged Christians in the western hemisphere to try to gain insights into Oriental philosophy and mysticism. He was killed in an accident while in Bangkok to visit the Dalai Lama (leader of the Tibetan Buddhists).

ICT FOR RESEARCH

Find out about the work of some Christian aid organisations.

Useful points to check:
- The origins of the organisation: Who? When? Where?
- Is it linked mostly with one denomination or with many?
- What are its aims, short-term and long-term?
- What does it do and where?

Find out about a recent project.

Paul describes the Church as one body and explains why members are concerned when others are suffering

The body is a unit, though it is made up of many parts; and though all its parts are many, they form one body. So it is with Christ. For we were all baptised by one Spirit into one body – whether Jews or Greeks, slave or free – and we were all given the one Spirit to drink. Now the body is not made up of one part but of many.

If one part suffers, every part suffers with it; if one part is honoured, every part rejoices with it. (I Corinthians 12:12–14, 26)

As Christian communities and churches of various denominations develop in many different countries, new challenges continue to meet them. Christians turn to the Bible, especially the New Testament, and try to apply the principles of love God and love your neighbour in a changing world. Christians believe that God is compassionate and therefore to carry out God's work on earth Christians must show compassion. Inevitably this means that Christians should not love and help only other Christians. They should show love to everybody. Jesus taught in the parable of the Good Samaritan (Luke 10:25–37) that every person is our neighbour.

All Christians are called to witness in their daily living. Part of the witness is loving and helping other people, Christians **and** non-Christians.

Some Christians work full-time or do voluntary unpaid work for Christian charities. Some work for charities, such as Oxfam, which are secular, or for causes such as Amnesty International. Some Christians give practical financial help such as donating money to charities. They see this as part of stewardship of their money.

Different ways of helping others can involve giving time, talents, prayer, and sympathy.

Many Christians feel that God has taught them to care for the whole of creation and that includes being kind to animals and being trustworthy stewards of the environment.

Many Christians also see that collective action is needed and they happily work alongside members of other faiths.

CHRISTIAN TEACHING ABOUT CHARITY AND CONCERN FOR OTHERS

CHARITY

The word charity comes from the Latin word 'caritas'. In English, charity tends to make people think of giving alms to the poor as a sort of duty or obligation. The Latin caritas is a translation of the New Testament Greek word *agape*, the word used in the hymn about love in 1 Corinthians 13. In the English language the one word 'love' covers all sorts of emotions, including sentimental sexual love. Perhaps this reflects the idea that all types of love – even the love for an animal – spring from the same deep emotional source.

The Greeks had many words for love. Scholars refer to 'storge' which is simply liking something, 'eros' which is sexual physical attraction, and to 'philos' and 'adelphos' which are friendly, brotherly or family love. The word *agape* means unselfish love. It seeks the welfare of the other person. It is the love of God flowing through people to others. Paul describes this love in 1 Corinthians 13. He says that it is the greatest of the spiritual gifts and will last through eternity.

In the early Church, besides celebrating the Eucharist, Christians used to meet together to share a meal. Because of the love and fellowship expressed in sharing it was called the agape feast, the love feast.

If I speak in the tongues of men and of angels, but have not love, I am only a resounding gong or a clanging cymbal. If I have the gift of prophecy and can fathom all mysteries and all knowledge, and if I have a faith that can move mountains, but have not love, I am nothing. If I give all I possess to the poor and surrender my body to the flames, but have not love, I gain nothing.

Love is patient, love is kind. It does not envy, it does not boast, it is not proud. It is not rude, it is not self-seeking, it is not easily angered, it keeps no record of wrongs. Love does not delight in evil but rejoices with the truth. It always protects, always trusts, always hopes, always perseveres.

Love never fails. But where there are prophecies, they will cease; where there are tongues, they will be stilled; where there is knowledge, it will pass away. For we know in part and we prophesy in part, but when perfection comes, the imperfect disappears. When I was a child, I talked like a child, I thought like a child, I reasoned like a child. When I became a man, I put childish ways behind me. Now we see but a poor reflection as in a mirror; then we shall see face to face. Now I know in part; then I shall know fully, even as I am fully known.

And now these three remain: faith, hope and love. But the greatest of these is love.

(1 Corinthians 13)

When Jesus told his followers to love God and love their neighbour, he was quoting from the Jewish Scriptures. The greedy selfishness of the rich and their lack of concern for the poor had provoked prophets in the Old Testament and Jesus in the New Testament to condemn the religious leaders of their society.

The Christian Church in many countries and at different times of history has been condemned for greed, avarice and neglect of the poor.

Christianity is not against people having money and property but Jesus warned his followers not to worship money and not to be greedy, selfish and materialistic (see Chapter 8 for biblical teaching about wealth and material possessions).

Christians believe that everything which they possess has been given to them by God in trust. They are not the owners; they are stewards.

Christians should be willing to sacrifice everything they have if God commands it. This includes not only material possessions but also worldly ambitions.

Helping others is a Christian duty. Help should be given with sincere intention and in gratitude for being in a position to give to others. Giving should be done with humility. Jesus said that it should be so secret that the left hand should not know what the right hand is doing.

FOR DISCUSSION

When you give something away, you become richer. Is this true?

In the western world, lottery money is used to fund all sorts of charitable causes. Christians differ in their attitudes to the lottery. Do you think Christians should or should not be involved in the lottery? Give reasons.

John answered, 'The man with two tunics should share with him who has none, and the one who has food should do the same.' (Luke 3:11)

What good is it, my brothers, if a man claims to have faith but has no deeds? Can such faith save him?

Suppose a brother or sister is without clothes and daily food. If one of you says to him, 'Go, I wish you well; keep warm and well fed,' but does nothing about his physical needs, what good is it? In the same way, faith by itself, if it is not accompanied by action, is dead.

(James 2:14–17)

John the Baptist was the cousin of Jesus. John was baptising Jews so they would be spiritually clean and ready for the Kingdom of God. John said they were relying on the fact that they were brought up as Jews. They had become proud of being Jews and they had forgotten their responsibilities to live as God wanted them to live. He said it was important that people should show that their repentance was genuine. They could wash away the past and start again. He also said that if they were serious about it, they should change their way of life.

The example in the verse says if you have two lots of clothes, give one away. The same goes for food.

Repentance means being truly sorry. Everybody makes mistakes. You might be sorry for things you have done which are wrong but also for things you did not do which you should have done.

FOR DISCUSSION

- Does John want people to give up everything?
- Does this sharing apply only to clothes and food?
- What does John say the tax collectors and the soldiers should do in the next verses? Does this advice help to show the meaning of verse 10 for Christians today?
- John goes on to say that a greater person will baptise not with water but with the Holy Spirit. Does that mean that John's baptism does not count as important any more?

There is a question that runs through the Bible. It is, 'What shall we do to be saved?' In both testaments, all sorts of people in all sorts of situations ask more or less this same question. Some religious people think the answer is that they should be righteous, law abiding and good. (Look at Psalm 1 for the poetic description of the righteous person.)

Christians accept that human beings find it very hard to be righteous or good.

Even when their actions are good, some Christians feel their motives are wrong or they know they felt resentful or even proud because of the effort they had to make.

FOR DISCUSSION

John Wesley, the founder of Methodism, once came down from the pulpit having given a terrific sermon. A lady commented how excellent the sermon had been and John Wesley said, 'Thank you madam. The Devil has told me so already.'

What did he mean?

Christian teaching says that salvation does not come from being good but by simply believing in Jesus. For some early Christians this idea was such a relief that they did not pay much attention to practical Christian living. To them, belief was all that mattered. Doing good deeds was to miss the point.

Paul in his letters to the churches kept reminding them that though they were saved by faith, it was important to show their faith in their daily life. Their good deeds would not buy them salvation but were the inevitable results of being true to the Christian faith and obvious signs that the Holy Spirit was working in them.

Luke the gospel writer had travelled with Paul. He must have met the same infectious enthusiasm among the congregations in the churches. The teaching from John the Baptist given in Luke 3:11 was very relevant to the early Christians. In some ways the teaching is very straightforward and simple. It is a reminder that faith must be put into action.

THINKING POINT

Read James 2:14–17.

How far do you think these verses are:
- addressing the same situation as Luke 3:11?
- giving the same advice?
- relevant to the Church today?

FOR DISCUSSION

Consider how far the following statements are true:
- Jesus in the Sermon on the Mount said that motives are important (see page 27).
- Christianity is more concerned with motives and intentions than with actions.
- Christianity from the start was for Jews and Gentiles, for rich and poor, for slave and free, for male and female.
- Protestantism encouraged individuals to read the scriptures for themselves and that opened the door to further splits in the Church.
- People who set themselves the highest standard of behaviour always aim for the highest but often they fail so they should have been more realistic in their aims.
- Wanting the best stops people appreciating the good.

THINKING POINT

Consider the topics you have discussed. How far is each a source of potential strength or of potential weakness for Christianity in making a helpful impact on the modern world?

RITES OF PASSAGE

Most societies have rites of passage. These are ceremonies which mark important stages in a person's life. They are celebrations involving the individual, the family and the community.

Most religions also have rites of passage. The ceremonies have religious significance and reflect the beliefs of the people.

BAPTISM/DEDICATION OF AN INFANT AND THE NURTURE OF THE YOUNG

To Christians, every child is a gift from God. Naturally, most Christian families attend a service to thank God for their child. They want God to bless and protect their child.

Roman Catholic and Orthodox Churches baptise babies. This practice is called infant baptism. The Lutherans, the Anglicans, the Methodists and the United Reformed Church do the same. The rite of baptism marks the entry of a new believer to the Church and to their local Christian community. Some Protestant Christian denominations believe that people should only be baptised when they themselves are old enough to know what they are doing. In those Churches, the couples take their baby to church for the minister to pray for God's blessing on the baby in a service of Dedication.

A main feature of services or ceremonies involving babies is the naming of the child. All rites of passage become a two-way mixture of religion and local culture. In western culture, the long association with Christianity has led to the first name of a person being 'the Christian name'.

Light is used as a symbol in infant baptism. It symbolises Jesus is the Light of the World. He told his followers to let their light shine.

Water is used in many religions. Water is essential to life. Water cleanses and purifies.

Ritual washing already existed in Judaism. Gentile proselytes who converted to Judaism were baptised in rivers, lakes or the sea. Communities like the Essenes of Qumran practised full immersion. John the Baptist was baptising people to repentance in the River Jordan. Christians who practise full immersion say they are following Jesus through the waters of baptism. From the beginning baptism seems to have been the ceremony for admitting people to the Church.

In Acts 8 Philip meets an Ethiopian who is travelling back home in a chariot and is reading aloud from Isaiah 53. Philip takes the opportunity to preach about Jesus. The Ethiopian is converted to Christianity and he says:

> *'Look, here is water. Why shouldn't I be baptised?'*
> (Acts 8:36)

Matthew ends his gospel with the Great Commission:

> *Therefore go and make disciples of all nations, baptising them in the name of the Father and of the Son and of the Holy Spirit, and teaching them to obey everything I have commanded you. And surely I am with you always, to the very end of the age.* (Matthew 28:19–20)

Nobody is sure when the first babies were baptised. In Acts 16, Lydia in Philippi and the Philippian jailer were baptised with their families and some argue that there would have been children in the household.

Tertullian complained about the baptism of babies in the second century so it was obviously a common practice by then. It was the belief in Original Sin that led to the Church baptising infants. The belief is that everyone is born in a state of sin which can only be removed by baptism. The Church was ensuring that the children were part of the saved community.

Christian parents are expected to bring up their children to love God and to live according to the teachings and principles of the Christian faith. They may take their children to church services and teach them to pray at home. Most of all, they must love their children.

> *People were bringing little children to Jesus to have him touch them, but the disciples rebuked them. When Jesus saw this, he was indignant. He said to them, 'Let the little children come to me, and do not hinder them, for the kingdom of God belongs to such as these. I tell you the truth, anyone who will not receive the kingdom of God like a little child will never enter it.' And he took the children in his arms, put his hands on them and blessed them.*
> (Mark 10:13–16)

Children can be badly behaved but it is their innocence, simplicity and dependency which can provide a lesson for adults.

> *He took a little child and had him stand among them. Taking him in his arms, he said to them, 'Whoever welcomes one of these little children in my name welcomes me; and whoever welcomes me does not welcome me but the one who sent me.'*
>
> *'And if anyone causes one of these little ones who believe in me to sin, it would be better for him to be thrown into the sea with a large millstone tied around his neck.'* (Mark 9:36–37, 42)

Not only the parents, but the godparents and the whole Christian community have a duty to children to bring them up in the Christian faith.

Christians believe that children need to be taught right from wrong. Some Christians send their children to church schools or to Sunday schools but the greatest education is the example set by the Christian parents. Parenting is an important part of family life.

THINKING POINT

- If you were a godparent of a Christian child what would you feel you need to do so that he or she might know God's love and understand the Christian faith?
- Is basic Christianity simple and easy enough for a child to understand?
- Look up Proverbs 13:24. Some Christian parents have used this verse to justify corporal punishment. How do you think parents can best discipline their children and encourage them to have respect for others and for their environment?

BELIEVER'S BAPTISM/CONFIRMATION

Baptism has been important in Christianity from the start but Christians have different views from each other about the significance of baptism.

Some Christians, like in the Baptist Churches, see baptism as an outward witness that a person has made a decision to commit their life to Christ. The full immersion in water symbolises the washing away of the old sinful life and the rising to new life in the power of the Holy Spirit.

Saul of Tarsus was baptised after his conversion to Christianity.

> *Immediately, something like scales fell from Saul's eyes, and he could see again. He got up and was baptised.* (Acts 9:18)

He wrote about the significance of baptism in a letter to the Christians in Roman:

> *Or don't you know that all of us who were baptised into Christ Jesus were baptised into his death? We were therefore buried with him through baptism into death in order that, just as Christ was raised from the dead through the glory of the Father, we too may live a new life.* (Romans 6:3–4)

Most who practise infant baptism see it as a sacrament which channels God's grace and blessing to a person's soul. As soon as the child is old enough to confirm the promises that were made by parents and godparents, he or she will join a confirmation class. Then the candidates will go to a confirmation service presided over by a bishop.

The anointing with oil at confirmation and the laying on of hands are important parts of the service.

The gift of the Holy Spirit is believed to be given during the confirmation service just like the Holy Spirit was given at Pentecost to the first Christians.

Both believers' baptism and confirmation are significant rites for the individual. The important point is that both rites are connected with the gift of the Holy Spirit. In public, the individual has witnessed to acceptance of the Christian faith and has made full commitment to living as a Christian in the power of the Holy Spirit.

Jesus told a man called Nicodemus in John 3 that no one can see the kingdom of God unless they are born again of water and the spirit.

THE MARRIAGE CEREMONY

Jesus attended a Jewish wedding at Cana in Galilee. Look up John 2:1–10.

The only necessary items for a marriage ceremony are:

- a bride and bridegroom who make certain legal statements
- witnesses
- someone who is authorised to conduct the wedding.

The only words that have to be said are the vows made between the bride and groom and a response by the person officiating.

The vows usually go something like this:

I, Peter, take you, Jane
(I, Jane, take you, Peter)
To be my wife (husband)
To have and to hold
From this day forward;
For better, for worse,
For richer, for poorer,
In sickness and in health,
To love and to cherish,
Til death us do part, according to God's holy law;
And this is my solemn vow.

The person officiating declares that Peter and Jane are now man and wife and adds the statement:

'That which God has joined together, let man not divide.'

Then the officiator addresses the people present:

'In the presence of God, and before the people here present, Peter and Jane have given their consent and made their marriage vows to each other. They have declared their marriage by the joining of hands and the giving and receiving of a ring and I therefore proclaim that they are husband and wife.'

Jesus described God's intention for marriage:

'It was because your hearts were hard that Moses wrote you this law,' Jesus replied. 'But at the beginning of creation God "made them male and female". For this reason a man will leave his father and mother and be united to his wife, and the two will become one flesh. So they are no longer two, but one. Therefore what God has joined together, let man not separate.'

(Mark 10:5–9)

Christians believe that marriage is the proper relationship in which:

- to have sexual intercourse
- to bear children
- to give mutual support.

All Christian denominations teach that marriage is intended to be a life-long commitment. The vows that are made are meant to be taken seriously.

The couple should not enter into marriage 'carelessly, lightly, or selfishly, but reverently, responsibly and after serious thought'.

In the Sermon on the Mount Jesus spoke about divorce (see Chapter 1 for commentary on Matthew 5:31–32) and most Christians interpret this teaching to mean that divorce is wrong. In the Roman Catholic Church divorce is not allowed. Couples who get divorced are not excommunicated but they cannot join in the sacramental life of the church, like taking the Eucharist. Sometimes couples are given an annulment which means that their marriage is regarded as never having taken place. The reasons why it might be declared null are:

- the marriage was not consummated sexually
- the couple were too young to understand
- either partner was mentally ill and did not understand.

The Orthodox Churches do not encourage divorce but a bishop has authority to grant a divorce and if the divorced people want to marry someone else later, the Orthodox Church will bless the marriage. This is particularly for the sake of the 'innocent' person in a divorce. Since 1966 the Church of England has taught that divorce is acceptable and since 1981 has agreed to allow divorced people to remarry. Most Protestant Churches believe it is the role of the Church to help people who have failed rather than to condemn them and that people should not be forced to live alone if a new marriage would give them the opportunity of finding happiness.

In the modern world, particularly in western culture and in big cities, many couples cohabit. They live together without getting married. The Roman Catholic Church is against cohabitation or any situation which includes a couple having sex outside marriage. Some Protestant Christians accept that cohabitation is seen as an option for many people today but they still believe that living together outside marriage is falling short of what God wanted.

Another issue on which Christian opinions are divided is homosexuality. A homosexual is attracted to members of the same sex. A heterosexual is attracted to people of the opposite sex. The Old Testament says that homosexuality is wrong and some people believe it was the reason God destroyed the cities of Sodom and Gomorrah in Genesis 14. In New Testament times homosexuality was more acceptable in Greek and Roman culture than it was to the Jews and some commentators think this is why New Testament writers such as Paul made a point of condemning it when giving advice to young Christian Churches.

Statistics indicate that approximately one in 14 people is gay. Female homosexuals are usually known as lesbians but both men and women describe themselves as gay. Laws have been passed in many countries to protect the rights of gay people and attitudes have similarly become more liberal in parts of the Christian Church. There is a Lesbian and Gay Christian Movement. For many years the Church has not condemned people for having feelings of attraction towards the same sex, as long as there is no physical sexual activity. Clergy of many denominations are willing to accept homosexuals and homosexual couples in their congregations but only the Society of Friends (Quakers) fully accept homosexuals who are sexually active.

THE ROLE OF THE FAMILY

Some individuals feel called to abstain from sexual activity and family life to dedicate themselves to prayer or to a religious cause. In the early days the Church seems to have valued celibacy (being unmarried and having no sexual relationships). They were difficult times for the Church and also, according to some theologians, many Christians were expecting the second coming of Jesus.

Paul recommended celibacy.

Now for the matters you wrote about: It is good for a man not to marry. But since there is so much immorality, each man should have his own wife, and each woman her own husband. The husband should fulfil his marital duty to his wife, and likewise the wife to her husband. The wife's body does not belong to her alone but also to her husband. In the same way, the husband's body does not belong to him alone but also to his wife.

I wish that all men were as I am. But each man has his own gift from God; one has this gift, another has that.

To the married I give this command (not I, but the Lord): A wife must not separate from her husband. But if she does, she must remain unmarried or else be reconciled to her husband. And a husband must not divorce his wife.

(1 Corinthians 7: 1–4, 7, 10–11)

There is a legend that Paul was on his travels with a lady called Thecla but this is from a sixth-century Coptic manuscript. There is a tradition that the Christian Church in Spain was founded by Paul and Thecla in 60 CE at Tarraco. Most theologians regard these stories as fictional because, from the New Testament, it seems that Paul was very aware of the dangers of the temptations of the flesh.

Peter and some of the other disciples of Jesus were married. Jesus was celibate, as far as we know. Jesus, however, was Jewish and Judaism has always valued family life. Traditionally the man's duty is to go out to work to support the family and the woman's duty is to bring up the children and look after the house.

> A wife of noble character who can find?
> She is worth far more than rubies.
> Her husband has full confidence in her
> and lacks nothing of value.
> She brings him good, not harm,
> all the days of her life.
>
> She is clothed with strength and dignity;
> she can laugh at the days to come.
> She speaks with wisdom,
> and faithful instruction is on her tongue.
> (Proverbs 31:10–12, 25–26)

Christians regard the family as the essential building block upon which religious and moral societies are founded. The role of Mary mother of Jesus is an important part of Christian teaching and devotion in many denominations around the world.

In some countries, extended families continue to exist with elderly grandparents living in the same house as the rest of the family unit, such as parents and children. Other relatives, who do not live in the same house, may live very close and children will grow up surrounded by grandparents, aunts, uncles and other members of the family. Traditional Christian family values seem appropriate in these cultures. Everyone has a role to play and everyone is valuable. The importance of women is shown in the fact that in the New Testament the Church is described as the bride of Christ.

The family is seen by Paul in the New Testament as a parallel to the authoritarian structure of the church.

> Wives, submit to your husbands as to the Lord. For the husband is the head of the wife as Christ is the head of the church, his body, of which he is the Saviour. Now as the church submits to Christ, so also wives should submit to their husbands in everything.
>
> Husbands, love your wives, just as Christ loved the church and gave himself up for her. . .
> (Ephesians 5:22–25)

The role of women changed dramatically in the twentieth century. Traditionally the procreation and rearing of children has been a main purpose of marriage for many Christians. Nowadays, however, even Roman Catholic theologians talk more of mutual love and responsibility. The declaration of Pope Paul VI in 1968 reiterating the traditional prohibition of artificial forms of contraception and birth control has caused much debate. Many Christians feel that Christianity must adapt to meet the needs of people in a changing world. People move around their country and around the world because of their employment. Families become fragmented. Individuals depend on their friends and workmates and these become a surrogate alternative family.

> While Jesus was still talking to the crowd, his mother and brothers stood outside, wanting to speak to him. Someone told him, 'Your mother and brothers are standing outside, wanting to speak to you.'
>
> He replied to him, 'Who is my mother, and who are my brothers?' Pointing to his disciples, he said, 'Here are my mother and my brothers. For whoever does the will of my Father in heaven is my brother and sister and mother.'
> (Matthew 12:46–50)

One of the Ten Commandments is 'Honour your father and mother'. Paul quotes this commandment in Ephesians 6:1–4.

Children, obey your parents in the Lord, for this is right. 'Honour your father and mother' – which is the first commandment with a promise – 'that it may go well with you and that you may enjoy long life on the earth.' Fathers, do not exasperate your children; instead, bring them up in the training and instruction of the Lord.

FUNERAL RITES, AND BELIEFS ABOUT DEATH AND DYING, LIFE AFTER DEATH

There are differences in the way funeral rites are observed because rituals vary according to the customs of the country in which the Christian has lived. The first crematorium was actually built in Washington Pennsylvania, USA in 1876. In the United Kingdom, Protestant non-conformists have accepted cremation since it was first made legal in England in 1884. Though many Protestant Christians supported the idea of cremation, many Anglican and Roman Catholic Christians continued to prefer burial of the coffin in the ground. They wanted the bodies to be intact for the resurrection of the dead from their graves at the Day of Judgement. In recent years, the Roman Catholic Church has announced that cremation is not forbidden. For most Christians, the soul has always been more important than the body.

FUNERAL RITES

When Roman Catholics are seriously ill and might die, a priest hears their confession and gives absolution from their sins. Anointing of the Sick may also be done when people are ill. The sick are anointed with oil which is a symbol of healing. It is special oil which has been blessed by the bishop during Holy Week. Prayers are said for physical and spiritual healing.

During the funeral service, the Paschal Candle is put by the head of the coffin. This is a symbol of the resurrection of Jesus. Holy water is sprinkled on the coffin. This is a symbol of baptism, the first rite of passage when the person became part of the Church. Families sometimes arrange for a requiem mass where prayers are offered for the soul of the dead relative.

Roman Catholics believe souls await cleansing of their sins in purgatory before entering heaven.

There are five parts to the funeral service:

- The corpse is carried to the church in a doleful procession of clergy and mourners, intoning psalms and using purifying incense.
- The coffin is placed in the church and covered with a pall, and the Office of the Dead is recited or sung, with the constant repetition of the prayer: 'Eternal rest grant unto him, O Lord, and let perpetual light shine upon him.'
- Next, requiem mass is said or sung, as an offering for the repose of the soul of the deceased.
- After the mass follows the 'Absolution' of the dead person, in which the coffin is solemnly perfumed with incense and sprinkled with holy water.
- The corpse is then carried to consecrated ground and buried, while appropriate prayers are recited by the officiating priest.

In the past, funeral ceremonies in Europe were often very sombre with the use of black vestments and candles of unbleached wax and the solemn tolling of the church bell.

Changes in these rites, including the use of white vestments and the recitation of prayers emphasising the notions of hope and joy, were introduced into the Catholic liturgy following the second Vatican Council (1962–65).

BELIEFS ABOUT DEATH AND DYING

Life does not finish when we die, according to Christianity. Death is not the end. The real permanent life is eternal life. Eternal life goes on for ever but it is more than just carrying on living after death. It is not only everlasting life. It is also life that has quality and it begins in this life. Christians believe that anyone who has a relationship with God will live for ever because friendship with God can never die. Christians believe they will go to be with God and Jesus and with their departed loved ones in heaven. Eternal life is beyond human imagining. It is a whole new dimension of existence. Even family relationships will change beyond earthly experience.

Most Christians take comfort from the words of Jesus in John 14.

> Do not let your hearts be troubled. Trust in God; trust also in me. In my Father's house are many rooms; if it were not so, I would have told you. I am going there to prepare a place for you. And if I go and prepare a place for you, I will come back and take you to be with me that you also may be where I am.　　(John 14:1–3)

Christians do not believe in reincarnation. There is only the one life on earth for each person. Christian creeds declare that Christians believe in the resurrection of the body (see Chapter 1). By this they mean that, like Jesus rose from the dead, their bodies will rise at the last day, the Day of Judgement, at the end of time. Though the end of the world is described very dramatically in the Bible along with the rewards and punishments of the afterlife, many Christians consider the descriptions to be symbolic picture language. There are some Christians, however, who interpret such passages literally.

The readings at a Christian funeral service are usually from 1 Corinthians 15.

In an Orthodox church, grain is sometimes put on a dish on a table by where prayers are said for the dead. The grain is a symbol of the mystery of life and death. Paul said an ordinary seed does not grow out of the ground looking like a seed. It looks like something totally different. It is the same with the human body when it dies.

> So will it be with the resurrection of the dead. The body that is sown is perishable, it is raised imperishable; it is sown in dishonour, it is raised in glory; it is sown in weakness, it is raised in power; it is sown a natural body, it is raised a spiritual body.
> 　　(1 Corinthians 15:42–44a)

PRACTICE EXAMINATION QUESTIONS

1 (a) **Describe the work of one Christian religious community. (8 marks)**

You may choose any type of Christian community but it is important to identify the group whose work you are describing and to give some details about the projects or activities they do. It might be an organisation like Christian Aid, Cafod or Tear Fund which give short-term and long-term aid to people in need or it might be a monastic order or a community such as Corrymeela which tries to work for peace between Roman Catholics and Protestants in Northern Ireland.

(b) **Explain the Christian teachings found in Luke 3:11 and James 2:14–17. (7 marks)**

There is no need to quote the passages word for word but you are expected to show that you are familiar with the set text. Any sensible explanation about charity and concern for others is acceptable as long as it can be linked to the verses.

(c) **'Helping the poor is the most important religious practice.'**

Do you agree? Give reasons to support your opinion and show you have thought about different points of view. You must refer to Christianity in your answer. (5 marks)

Remember to refer to Christianity and to pay attention to the word 'most'. The questions are structured around the theme of helping the poor so you may find it useful to base your discussion on points you have made in the first two parts of the question.

2 (a) **Describe what is said and done at an infant baptism. (8 marks)**

An infant baptism may be described from any Christian denomination. It is wise to name the denomination. Some credit might be gained by describing christening gowns and crying babies but the main part of the answer should be the significant words spoken, e.g. promises by the parents and the godparents and the Trinitarian invocation by the priest as water is poured on the baby's head.

(b) Explain the meaning and importance of baptism for Christians. (7 marks)

You may wish to explain the meaning and importance of the baptism you have described, including any symbolism. You may, however, wish to explain the meaning of baptism in general and to refer to believer's baptism. Either approach is equally acceptable. It is the quality of the explanations which is important.

(c) 'You can be a Christian without being baptised.' Do you agree? Give reasons to support your opinion and show you have thought about different points of view. (5 marks)

There are many equally valid ways to approach this discussion. Try to think how different Christians might answer this. A good debate is likely to include consideration of the fact that for some Christians baptism is a sacrament. It may be useful to attempt to define what might be meant by a 'Christian'.

3 (a) Describe the making of vows at a Christian marriage ceremony and state what the vows mean. (8 marks)

Any Christian wedding service may be used. A brief description of the relevant part of the service is useful but the main focus should be the content of the vows that the couple are swearing before God.

(b) Explain how Christian teachings may help people solve problems in their family life. (7 marks)

Set passages from any part of the syllabus may be used or any other relevant Christian or Biblical teaching. There are many ways to approach the question. The examination requires candidates to be able to explain the relevance and application of religion. Practical examples of love, forgiveness and care will help your explanation. It may be useful to think of the vows that were made and link the teachings with issues of money, health and faithfulness.

(c) 'Only couples who attend a Christian place of

worship regularly should be allowed to be married there.'

Do you agree? Give reasons to support your opinion and show you have thought about different points of view. (5 marks)

You may wish to define the word 'regularly' during the discussion. Marriage is a rite of passage and you may wish to discuss Christian attitudes to the fact that in Britain for example some people only go to church when there are 'hatch, match and dispatch' occasions.

4 (a) Describe what is said and done at a Christian funeral. (8 marks)

Any Christian funeral service may be used but the description should be quite detailed. Note that both said and done are expected. The service does not need to be recited word for word but the general sense should be given of what is said.

(b) Explain how beliefs about the afterlife might affect the way Christians live. (7 marks)

People's beliefs do affect their lives. Some beliefs might make people fearful and might have a negative effect but religion also might bring hope and consolation when people are mourning and might encourage believers to live useful lives and to treat other people well.

(c) 'Religious people should welcome death.'

Do you agree? Give reasons to support your opinion and show you have thought about different points of view. You must refer to Christianity in your answer. (5 marks)

Consider what the range of Christian opinions might be before you start. You may wish to point out that it all depends on certain factors before a decision could be made about the statement. Often in discussions it is not as straightforward as saying, 'yes this is true because ...' or 'no this is not true because ...'. Different points of view do not have to be totally opposite. They could be a discussion of the sort of factors which should be taken into consideration. You may wish to query the use of one word in the statement. For example, in this question you may think that 'welcome' is not a totally appropriate word.

7

SACRED WRITINGS

For most of the world's religions there is a particular book, or several books, which are considered sacred. These books often contain the main beliefs of the religion, its history and teachings about how people should live their lives.

For the Jews these texts are called the Torah and the Tenakh, for Muslims it is the Qur'an, for Sikhs the Guru Granth Sahib Ji and Hindus and Buddhists also have books of teachings and history which hold a special place in their life and worship.

Sometimes these books are the writings of religious leaders from the past. In the case of the Guru Granth Sahib Ji it is a collection of the writings of the ten human Gurus from Guru Nanak Dev Ji to Guru Gobind Singh Ji. When Guru Gobind Singh Ji died he had decreed that in future there would be no more human gurus and that instead the Guru Granth Sahib Ji should be treated with the honour and respect which would have been shown to a human leader.

For Muslims, the Holy Qur'an contains the teachings which the Prophet Muhammad received from the angel Jibril. Muslims say that the Qur'an on earth is a copy of the first Qur'an which is in Paradise with Allah. Allah instructed Jibril to teach the Qur'an to Muhammad . The Prophet could not read or write so he learnt the Qur'an in sections and told it to his friends who wrote it down. Muslims believe that the copies of the Qur'an which they have today are identical to that dictated to Muhammad . The Qur'an was 'revealed' to Muhammad by Jibril and it is described as revealed scripture. This means that it comes directly from Allah and contains the words of Allah.

ICT FOR RESEARCH

Find out more about the sacred texts of two other religions

The Jews believe that the first five books of their scriptures, Genesis, Exodus, Leviticus, Numbers and Deuteronomy, which are called the Torah (Law), were given to Moses by God. These five books are also revealed scripture. They are written on special scrolls called the Sefer Torah and are shown great respect when they are carried around the synagogue and when people read from them.

The Bible is also believed by many Christians to be revealed scripture and many say that every word of the Bible is true.

The name 'Bible' comes from the Greek 'Biblia' which means 'books'. The Christian Bible is split into two main sections, the Old Testament and the New Testament.

The name Testament comes from a Latin word 'Testamentum' which means 'covenant'. People did not start calling the Jewish scriptures the Old Testament until after the life of Jesus. This was because Jesus made a New Covenant with his followers to replace the Old Covenant of the Jews.

THE OLD TESTAMENT

The Old Testament contains the same books as the Tenakh of the Jews but not in quite the same order.

The first five books of the Old Testament are the writings of the Torah and tell the early history of the Jews and their relationship with God as well as the laws which God wanted the Jews to follow and the covenants, or promises, which were made between the Jews and God.

The other books of the Old Testament contain various different types of literature including law, prophecy, poetry, liturgy and history. Sometimes the books contain more than one type of material. For example, the Book of Psalms is usually classified as poetry but many of the Psalms appear to have been used in worship by the Jews and so they can also be called liturgy, and the five books of the law also contain history and poetry.

Most of these books were originally written in Hebrew (though Ezra and Daniel were written in Aramaic) and this is the language in which Jesus would have learnt from them in the synagogue in Nazareth.

Aramaic is a language very similar to Hebrew. By the time of Jesus it had replaced Hebrew as the spoken language of the Jews.

Later, the Old Testament was translated into Greek, this was known as the Septuagint. This is from the Latin word 'septuaginta' which means 70. Tradition says that the High Priest in Jerusalem at the time of the Emperor Ptolemy II (309–246 BCE) chose 70 translators to create a Greek version of the scriptures.

The Septuagint contained an extra 15 books which were not part of the original Hebrew canon. The word 'canon', from the Greek 'kanwn' means a rule or a measuring rod. Its use means that people believed the books of the canon to be genuine.

These 15 books are now often referred to as the Apocrypha, a Latin word which means 'hidden'. The books are called hidden because people have not agreed whether they are a genuine part of the scriptures or not. Some of these appear in the Roman Catholic Bible whilst in some Protestant Bibles they are printed together between the Old and New Testaments. These books were probably written between 200 BCE and 100 CE. Some are history and some poetry, whilst *Bel and the Dragon* is really a detective story.

THINKING POINT

Try to find a copy of *Bel and the Dragon* and read it. What do you think was the original purpose of this book?

THE BOOKS OF THE APOCRYPHA

1 Esdras
2 Esdras
Tobit
Judith
The rest of Esther (Esther 10:4–10)
The Wisdom of Solomon
Ecclesiasticus
Baruch, with the Epistle of Jeremiah
The Song of the Three Holy Children (Daniel 3:24–90)
The History of Susanna (Daniel 13)
Bel and the Dragon (Daniel 14)
The Prayer of Manasseh
1 Maccabees
2 Maccabees

The way in which the books of the Bible are grouped together is different between the Hebrew Scriptures, the Roman Catholic Bible and Protestant Bible.

BOOKS OF THE BIBLE

TENAKH	ROMAN CATHOLIC BIBLE	PROTESTANT BIBLE
The Law	**The Pentateuch**	**The Pentateuch**
Genesis	Genesis	Genesis
Exodus	Exodus	Exodus
Leviticus	Leviticus	Leviticus
Numbers	Numbers	Numbers
Deuteronomy	Deuteronomy	Deuteronomy
The Prophets	**The Historical Books**	**The Historical Books**
Earlier Prophets	Joshua	Joshua
Joshua	Judges	Judges
Judges	Ruth	Ruth
1 Samuel	1 Samuel	1 Samuel
2 Samuel	2 Samuel	2 Samuel
1 Kings	1 Kings	1 Kings
2 Kings	2 Kings	2 Kings
Latter Prophets	1 Chronicles	1 Chronicles
Isaiah	2 Chronicles	2 Chronicles
Jeremiah	Ezra	Ezra
Ezekiel	Nehemiah	Nehemiah
Hosea	Tobit 1	Esther
Joel	Judith 1	
Amos	Esther	
Obadiah	1 Maccabees 1	
Jonah	2 Maccabees 1	
Micah		
Nahum		
Habakkuk		
Zephaniah		
Haggai		
Zechariah		
Malachi		
The Writings	**The Wisdom Books**	**The Poetical Books**
Psalms	Job	Job
Proverbs	Psalms	Psalms
Job	Proverbs	Proverbs

Song of Songs	Ecclesiastes	Ecclesiastes
Ruth	Song of Songs	Song of Solomon
Lamentations	Wisdom 1	
Ecclesiastes	Sirach 1	
Esther		
Daniel		
Ezra		
Nehemiah		
1 Chronicles		
2 Chronicles		

The Prophetical Books	**The Prophetical Books**
Isaiah	Isaiah
Jeremiah	Jeremiah
Lamentations	Lamentations
Baruch 1	Ezekiel
Ezekiel	Daniel
Daniel	Hosea
Hosea	Joel
Joel	Amos
Amos	Obadiah
Obadiah	Jonah
Jonah	Micah
Micah	Nahum
Nahum	Habakkuk
Habakkuk	Zephaniah
Zephaniah	Haggai
Haggai	Zechariah
Zechariah	Malachi
Malachi	

The actual order and choice of books in the Old Testament of the Bible was not finalised until the sixteenth century.

It is important to remember that Jesus was a Jew, and so were his first followers. Because of this, the Old Testament is still a very important part of the Bible.

One of the most important ideas in the Old Testament is the relationship between God and humanity. The prophets wrote about the coming of a Messiah, who would bring peace to the earth.

For to us a child is born,
to us a son is given,
and the government will be on his shoulders.
And he will be called
Wonderful Counsellor, Mighty God,
Everlasting Father, Prince of Peace.
Of the increase of his government and peace
there will be no end.
He will reign on David's throne
and over his kingdom,
establishing and upholding it
with justice and righteousness
from that time on and for ever.
The zeal of the LORD Almighty
will accomplish this.   (Isaiah 9:6–7)

Isaiah also wrote that this Messiah or Servant of God would suffer for the people's sins. Christians believe that this servant was Jesus.

ICT FOR RESEARCH

Look for some of the other references to the Messiah in the Old Testament. How far do you think Jesus was the Messiah the Old Testament writers were hoping for?

THE NEW TESTAMENT

The other part of the Christian Bible is the New Testament. This section contains the writings of the early Christians. Many of these books were written long after the events with which they are concerned and scholars still argue about the actual dates when they first appeared as written documents. It seems that, for many years, people handed on the stories by word of mouth – this is called 'oral tradition' – and that it was not until many years later that the books of the New Testament reached the form in which we know them today.

The canon or group of books which now form the New Testament was not agreed by the Church until 367 CE and at that time many other gospels and epistles were left out of the Bible because people were not convinced that they were genuine. These are known as the New Testament Apocrypha.

FOR DISCUSSION

Find out the names of some of the books which are found in the New Testament apocrypha.

The New Testament consists of 27 books:

THE GOSPELS	1 Thessalonians
Matthew	2 Thessalonians
Mark	1 Timothy
Luke	2 Timothy
John	Titus
	Philemon
Acts of the Apostles	Hebrews
	James
Epistles	1 Peter
Romans	2 Peter
1 Corinthians	1 John
2 Corinthians	2 John
Galatians	3 John
Ephesians	Jude
Philippians	Revelation (Apocalypse)
Colossians	

Saint Mathew from the Book of Kells.

MATTHEW, MARK, LUKE AND JOHN – THE FOUR GOSPELS

The word Gospel means 'good news'. It comes from the Old English 'godspel' and before that from the Greek 'euanggelion'. All four Gospels were probably written originally in Greek, with the authors making use of earlier Aramaic sources that held many of the actual words and sayings of Jesus.

The gospels give four differing accounts of the life and teachings of Jesus but do not attempt to give a biography. They are the products of the individual writers, whoever they were. Although they are called by the names of four of the disciples it seems very unlikely that these were the actual writers.

Two of the gospels, Matthew and Luke, begin with the birth of Jesus whilst the others start much later in his life. It is clear from reading the four accounts that we know very little about Jesus' life before he was 30.

FOR DISCUSSION

What exactly do we know about Jesus' life before he started to preach in Galilee?

The first three gospels are called the Synoptic Gospels because of their similar overall view of the material, while the fourth gospel is rather different and tends to be more theological in the way in which it handles the material about Jesus' life.

It is probable that they were all written within a hundred years of Jesus' death and existed in an oral tradition before that time. Therefore the details vary significantly from one book to the next. In the same way, there are sometimes disagreements in the text about the order in which events took place. This is particularly noticeable when people compare the accounts of the last days of Jesus' life from his arrival in Jerusalem and his resurrection on Easter Day. However, although there are differences in detail the message and teachings of Jesus remain essentially the same.

In the past, some scholars have tried to prove that the four accounts of Jesus' life can be put together without any discrepancies but this has proven to be very difficult.

IN YOUR NOTES

Draw a chart and plot what each gospel says about the events of Holy Week from Thursday until Sunday.

THE SYNOPTIC PROBLEM

Before the nineteenth century most people believed that Matthew was the earliest gospel to have been written, that Mark was a shortened form of Matthew and that Luke was the last, drawing on both Matthew and Mark for material.

However, more recently, scholars have looked closely at the text and have come up with a different theory. They believe that Mark is the earliest gospel. They also believe that the writers of Matthew and Luke had another source available. This source is now usually called Q (from the German word Quelle 'source').

FOR DISCUSSION

Try to find out more information about Q and the Synoptic Problem.

Q is thought to have been written in Aramaic and to have been a collection of sayings of Jesus. There are still some passages in the Bible where Jesus' words remain in Aramaic.

One is when Jesus brings a dead girl back to life.

When they came to the home of the synagogue ruler, Jesus saw a commotion, with people crying and wailing loudly. He went in and said to them, 'Why all this commotion and wailing? The child is not dead but asleep.' But they laughed at him.

> *After he put them all out, he took the child's father and mother and the disciples who were with him, and went in where the child was. He took her by the hand and said to her, 'Talitha koum!' (which means, 'Little girl, I say to you, get up!'). Immediately the girl stood up and walked around (she was twelve years old). At this they were completely astonished. He gave strict orders not to let anyone know about this, and told them to give her something to eat.* (Mark 5:38–43)

And another is when he is on the cross:

> *At the sixth hour darkness came over the whole land until the ninth hour. And at the ninth hour Jesus cried out in a loud voice, 'Eloi, Eloi, lama sabachthani?' (which means, 'My God, my God, why have you forsaken me?')* (Mark 15:33–34)

Other scholars also believe that Matthew had an additional document called 'M' which was not available to the writer of Luke.

ACTS OF THE APOSTLES TO REVELATION

The next book in the New Testament is the Acts of the Apostles. This takes the story of Jesus and the early Church forward from Luke's Gospel and it is often thought to be a simple continuation of that gospel. It tells the problems and debates of the early Church during the 30 years after the Ascension of Jesus and describes the arguments and persecutions which the disciples experienced in spreading the words of Christ.

The Epistles or Letters is the largest group of books in the New Testament. These were written by members of the early Church. Most of the epistles are of an earlier date than the Gospels and so they are the first information which we have about the Christianity and the Christian Church.

Traditionally the first 14 epistles are said to have been written by Paul but scholars think it is unlikely that they are all by the same person. Two appear to have been written by Peter and three by John. It is important to remember that some of the Epistles say that they were written to, for example, Timothy by Paul, others say the Letter of James or the Letter of John.

These writers were the earliest leaders of the Christian Church and wrote to places where there were communities of believers to support them and give them guidance.

The Epistles have always provided a base for the Christian way of life as they try to explain how to live according to the teachings of Jesus.

The last book in the New Testament is called The Revelation of St John or the Apocalypse. This is certainly one of the most difficult books of the Bible to understand.

The book begins:

> *The revelation of Jesus Christ, which God gave him to show his servants what must soon take place. He made it known by sending his angel to his servant John, who testifies to everything he saw – that is, the word of God and the testimony of Jesus Christ. Blessed is the one who reads the words of this prophecy, and blessed are those who hear it and take to heart what is written in it, because the time is near.* (Revelation 1:1–3)

It is addressed to: 'the seven churches in the province of Asia'.

The author of Revelation is probably not the same man who wrote John's Gospel nor the Epistles of John.

The most important thing about Revelation is that it contains a vision or dream of an early

Christian in which, in mysterious and almost magical language, he gives an impression of what the future of the Christian Church will be. It describes the Day of Judgement and what will happen on the earth and in heaven at that time.

For many hundreds of years priests and scholars have tried to understand this book and to explain it to Christians. It continues to be valuable because it shows the struggle between good and evil with evil triumphing and also the idea that, in the end, God's followers will be triumphant.

Many artists, writers and film makers have used passages from the Book of Revelation as inspiration for their work.

BIBLE TRANSLATIONS

In the fifth century, St Jerome built a monastery in Bethlehem and lived there while he translated the Old Testament into Latin from the original Hebrew. Together with the translation of the New Testament from Greek into Latin, which he had carried out earlier, this forms the Vulgate Bible which is the standard text used by the Roman Catholic Church.

The Bible has since been translated into many languages. Parts of the Bible were already in Coptic, Syriac and Gothic before Jerome produced the Vulgate.

The first translation into English took place in the seventh century when a monk called Caedmon translated part of the Vulgate. Bede d.735 CE

translated the gospels into English. Then in the ninth century, King Alfred translated parts of the Ten Commandments and the Psalms.

The Lindisfarne Gospels c.950 CE had both Latin and English texts. More material was produced in the tenth century by Aelfric, Abbot of Eynsham and in the fourteenth century the Psalms were translated by William of Shoreham and also by Richard Rolle.

John Wycliffe (c.1329–84) led the first translation of the entire Bible from Latin into English. The New Testament was published in 1380 and the Old Testament in 1382. Wycliffe felt that it was his duty to make the Bible available to everyone so that they could read and hear it for themselves and not just in the way in which the Church interpreted it. He then organised a group of poor parishioners, known as Lollards, to travel across England preaching Christian truths and reading the Scriptures in English.

A revision of this translation was produced by John Purvey in 1388.

The problem with these translations was that they were all taken from the Vulgate not from the original languages.

In the sixteenth century, a scholar called William Tyndale wanted to make a new translation saying to the priests who opposed him, 'If God spare my life, ere many years, I will cause a boy that driveth the plough to know more of the Scripture than thou dost.'

He met so much opposition in London that he went to Germany. There he translated the New

Tyndale's Bible, 1536

Testament from Greek in 1525. As copies of his translation arrived in England, the Church attempted to burn them but was unsuccessful.

He then began a translation of the Old Testament from the Hebrew but was captured in 1535 and burnt at the stake in 1536 – all because he wanted people to read the Bible in their own language.

Miles Coverdale was an assistant of Tyndale. By the time he had completed the Pentateuch in 1537, the Reformation had taken place in England and an English Bible was welcomed by the king, Henry VIII.

Thomas Matthew (John Rogers) a friend of Tyndale, then compiled a complete Bible in English from the translations of Tyndale and Coverdale. This was approved by the King and printed to be placed in all churches. It is often called the Great Bible, because of its size and cost.

Under the rule of Queen Mary, who wished to make England a Roman Catholic country again, John Rogers was executed and Coverdale had to flee to Geneva.

In Geneva, the English exiles commissioned William Whittingham (c. 1524–79) to make an English translation of the New Testament for them. This was not popular in the Church of England, again needing an English translation, because of the influence of John Calvin (see page 67) in the work.

Therefore, the Church ordered a revision of the Great Bible which was eventually published in 1568 as the Bishops' Bible.

When James VI of Scotland became James I of England he called a meeting of Church leaders to produce a new translation of the Bible.

In 1607, 50 scholars and several committees worked on the project. They worked using the original texts, the Bishops' Bible, the translations of Tyndale, Matthew and Coverdale as well as the Great Bible and the Geneva Bible.

The preface to the King James Bible says: 'Truly, good Christian reader, we never thought from the beginning that we should need to make a new translation, nor yet to make of a bad one a good one . . . but to make a good one better, or out of many good ones one principal good one'.

The King James Bible is now known as the Authorised Version and has been the basis for many of the translations which have appeared since then.

THINKING POINT

Why do you think it is important for people to be able to read the Bible in their own language?
Try to find out why the Roman Catholic Church did not want the Bible to be translated from Latin.

The Bible is the most important and holy book for Christians. They believe that it is the 'Word of God', and a way in which God communicates to humanity.

Christians try to understand the messages of the Bible, and to live their lives according to its teachings.

In every church service there are readings from the Bible and often the sermon explores the teachings in the passage which has been read.

The Bible usually has a special place of importance in a church. It is often kept on a special stand called a lectern.

During the Eucharist, there are sometimes three readings: one from the Old Testament, one from the Epistles or the book of Revelation, and one from the Gospels.

Some Christians read the Bible at home every day and some Christian families read passages together or in small groups. Christians believe that the Bible contains the teachings they need to understand God and follow Jesus' teachings.

Christians from different traditions give different weight to the importance of the Scriptures.

In very general terms the Protestant Churches tend to place more stress on the Bible than does, for example, the Roman Catholic Church, where the Bible is interpreted through the tradition of Church teaching.

Some Christians are described as 'fundamentalists'. They believe that the Bible 'revealed' and is the actual word of God. Therefore every word of it is true as it stands. They think that everything in the Bible must have happened in exactly the way that it is described. They believe that if scientists or historians have different understandings of the world, it is the Bible which is right and the people who are wrong, because they think that people make mistakes but God never does. They might have difficulties when passages in the Bible seem to be contradicted by modern evidence.

Other Christians say that although the writing is inspired by God it was nevertheless created by human beings and therefore may have mistakes in it and may need to be interpreted for the age in which it is used.

Some Christians believe that parts of the Bible are not literally true as fact but are true in other ways, perhaps as myths, as hymns, or as poems. They may believe that sometimes the Bible shows a view of the world that is outdated now. For example, they might think that the Bible's attitude to women is not appropriate for the modern world, or that scientists have a better understanding than the Biblical writers of the origins of the world. These Christians might have difficulties in knowing which parts of the Bible are actually true and which are not.

FOR DISCUSSION

Why do you think that these different approaches to the Bible may be of advantage or disadvantage to Christians?

PRACTICE EXAMINATION QUESTIONS

1 (a) **Describe how Christians show respect for the Bible in a place of worship. (*8 marks*)**

In this question you need to consider how the Bible is used and treated in a place of public worship. You can describe the different ways in which it is treated, e.g. reading it from a special lectern, carrying it in procession, saying special words or phrases before and after a reading.

(b) **Explain how Christians might use the teaching of the Bible in their daily lives. (*7 marks*)**

Here you need to focus on the 'teachings' of the Bible. It might help people to get on with others better. It might give them hope for the future. It might show them examples of how they should lead their lives.

(c) **'Christianity would not exist without the Bible.'**
Do you agree? Give reasons to support your answer and show that you have thought about different points of view. (*5 marks*)

In this question you have to give different viewpoints. You have learnt in this chapter that the New Testament existed for some time without being written down, so you could argue that Christianity might exist without the Bible. On the other hand, it is possible that if the teachings of Christianity were still passed on by oral tradition, many of them would have become very corrupted after 2000 years.

2 (a) **Describe how daily Bible reading might affect a Christian's life. (*8 marks*)**

Answers should consider the practice of reading verses from the Bible every day whether alone or with other people and how doing this might mean that the teachings of the Bible can strengthen people's faith and help them in their lives.

(b) **Why are the gospels and epistles so important to Christians? (*7 marks*)**

In answering this question you need to show why both of these collections of books are important. The gospels are important because they tell us almost all we know about the life of Jesus and contain his teachings and accounts of the miracles he performed. The epistles are important because they are letters to the members of the early Church, explaining how they should live. Also, the epistles are the very first Christian writings.

(c) **'Reading the Bible is the best way to find out what God wants.'**
Do you agree? Give reasons to support your answer and show you have thought about different points of view. You must refer to Christianity in your answer. (*5 marks*)

While it is true that Christians believe that the Bible contains teachings about how God wants people to behave and what they should believe, other people might say that they can learn about what God wants through prayer and meditation.

3 (a) **Describe what types of literature the Bible contains. (*8 marks*)**

In answering this question you are not expected to give a complete list of the contents of the Bible but you should be able to write about the main types of writing found in the Old Testament and the New Testament and give examples of these.

(b) **Explain how and why Christians might show respect for the Bible in their daily lives. (*7 marks*)**

Most people would say that Christians show respect for the Bible in their everyday lives by following its teachings. You need to explain this and also say 'why' they do this. The answer here is likely to be because they believe that the Bible is the word of God and so contains God's teachings.

(c) **'Christians should pay more attention to the New Testament than to the Old Testament.'**
Do you agree? Give reasons to support your answer and show that you have thought about different points of view. (5 marks)
Christians probably do pay more attention to the teachings of the New Testament rather than the Old Testament because it contains the stories and teachings of Jesus. However, Jesus was a Jew and he was very much influenced by the Jewish Scriptures, the Old Testament, and you need to reflect this in your answer.

4 (a) **Describe how Christians might use the Bible in Sunday services. (8 marks)**
Any place of worship from any Christian denomination may be used in the description but it is sensible to identify which denomination it is. The Sunday services might need to be described briefly but the focus of the answer is the use of the Bible in the services.

(b) **Explain why young Christians might find it helpful to study the Bible together. (8 marks)**
You are being asked to consider why the Bible is important and relevant to Christians and why group study might benefit young Christians and how they might apply the teachings of the Bible. Think of the Bible passages you have studied during the course. Might these provide examples for you to quote?

(c) **'Holy books should not be translated into modern everyday language.'**
Do you agree? Give reasons to support your answer and show that you have thought about different points of view. You must refer to Christianity in your answer. (5 marks)
Before you begin, consider what various Christians might say. All Christians are glad that their scriptures were not left in Hebrew and Greek but were translated so the whole world could read the Bible. Bible translation was a big adventure story; today the Bible is in virtually all the languages of the world. Some Christians, however, wish the Bible and church services had been left in Latin and others wish the King James' Authorised Version in English had not been translated into so many modern versions. What reasons might people have for these opinions? How far do you agree with them?

8

RELIGION, THE MEDIA AND ENTERTAINMENT

Media can be television, radio, videos, DVDs, CD-ROMs, newspapers, magazines, books, posters, advertisements, computers and the internet, art, music, dance and drama, and sport. It can, in fact, be anything that is the medium for communicating with other people.

Humans have always given each other information, demonstrated new methods of doing things, communicated their feelings, made each other laugh and shared their opinions and beliefs. Every day in our modern world new ways of doing these things are developed.

In all religions and in all cultures there are some people who say that the media is a bad influence and that young people especially are misled by the media.

There are some religious people who welcome new inventions in the media and communication. They feel that modern technology will improve the quality of life for everyone and they see mass media as providing an opportunity to spread their beliefs.

There are, however, many religious people who have mixed feelings about the media and entertainment.

FOR DISCUSSION

What do you think are the advantages and disadvantages of modern media?

Which of these advantages and disadvantages might apply to the media from the point of view of Christians?

When Christians are deciding about an issue, they turn to various sources of authority:

- they read the Bible
- they take the advice of the Church and of their Christian friends
- they use their conscience and pray to God and ask to be guided by the Holy Spirit.

FOR DISCUSSION

Some religions have set rules to obey rather than general principles. Would that make life easier? What are the advantages and disadvantages of rules?

THE ISSUES

MONEY

Christians believe that God created the universe and it is good. They believe also that humans have a responsibility of stewardship over the material world. Some Christians may emphasise the potential for the positive use of material things. Other Christians may be concerned about the created world as a possible source of sin and temptation that can lead people away from concentrating on spiritual truths.

These differing attitudes may affect the way individual Christians approach issues concerning wealth and opportunities for physical work and leisure activities.

> *What is the chief end of man?*
> *To glorify God and to enjoy him forever. (The shorter catechism)*
>
> *So whether you eat or drink or whatever you do, do it all for the glory of God.* (1 Corinthians 10:31)

Christians all share the belief that the purpose of life is to glorify God whatever you may be doing. It follows that Christians should try to do their work conscientiously and use their leisure time constructively.

Sport is considered a healthy activity by most Christians and some football clubs owe their original existence to church rivalry in big cities. Of course, in those days many Christians would never have dreamed of playing football on Sundays, the Christian holy day. Some Christians, however, would have frowned on sport on any day, along with dancing, drama and all types of frivolous pleasure. They thought life was too serious to waste time on pastimes.

Some Protestant denominations were very suspicious of leisure activities. They took work seriously and tended to be thrifty about the use of money. To this day we use the term 'Protestant work ethic' to describe such an attitude to life. Some of these individuals and churches worked for social change. Some campaigned against slavery and for prison reform. They were concerned about the ills in society caused by poverty and disease.

> *Jesus said:*
> *'Do not store up for yourselves treasures on earth, where moth and rust destroy, and where thieves break in and steal. But store up for yourselves treasures in heaven, where moth and rust do not destroy, and where thieves do not break in and steal. For where your treasure is, there your heart will be also.'* (Matthew 6:19–21)

Jesus told his followers to put God first in their lives. Christians believe they must get their priorities right. They certainly should not live for making money.

Paul says that it is not money but the attitude to money which causes problems.

> *But godliness with contentment is great gain. For we brought nothing into the world, and we can take nothing out of it. But if we have food and clothing, we will be content with that. People who want to get rich fall into temptation and a trap and into many foolish and harmful desires that plunge men into ruin and destruction. For the love of money is a root of all kinds of evil. Some people, eager for money, have wandered from the faith and pierced themselves with many griefs.* (1 Timothy 6:6–10)

Here are some of the other biblical passages which might influence Christians concerning the use of money:

- Luke 12:13–21 parable of the Rich Fool
- Luke 16:19–31 parable of the Rich Man and Lazarus
- Luke 18:18–25 Jesus tells the rich young ruler to sell all he has and give it to the poor
- Mark 12:41–44 Jesus commends a widow's offering of small coins which are a large proportion of her income
- Matthew 25:14–30 parable of the Talents

- Acts 2:44–47 the example of sharing set by the early Church
- Acts 20:35 Paul quotes Jesus saying, 'It is more blessed to give than receive'
- 2 Corinthians 8:1–15 Paul advising about collecting for the poor
- Leviticus 25:14, 23, 35–36 Jewish law about lending to others and not charging interest.

For Christians, not only actions but thoughts and intentions are important. Caring too much about material things is like worshipping false gods. It is said that you may think you own the possessions but in the end they own you. Even poor people could be guilty of making idols of things they want but cannot afford.

In some churches, Christians give a tenth of their income to their religion each week. This money is used to support not only the local church but the work of Christians around the world. The gift of money is called a tithe.

A tithe of everything from the land, whether grain from the soil or fruit from the trees, belongs to the Lord; it is holy to the Lord. If a man redeems any of his tithe, he must add a fifth of the value to it. The entire tithe of the herd and flock – every tenth animal that passes under the shepherd's rod – will be holy to the Lord. He must not pick out the good from the bad or make any

substitution. If he does make a substitution, both the animal and its substitute become holy and cannot be redeemed. (Leviticus 27:30–33)

In the gospels Jesus criticised the Jewish leaders because they were extremely careful about paying their tithes but they neglected more important things like caring for other people and loving God.

Woe to you Pharisees, because you give God a tenth of your mint, rue and all other kinds of garden herbs, but you neglect justice and the love of God. You should have practised the latter without leaving the former undone. (Luke 11:42)

All Christians believe they should give some of their income to help others and there are many different ways they might do this.

Christians believe there is nothing wrong in having wealth, as long as it was earned in an honest way and it is used in a sensible way.

Whatever you do, work at it with all your heart as working for the Lord, not for men. (Colossians 3:23)

FOR DISCUSSION

It is a basic Christian principle that all Christians have a 'vocation', a 'calling', whatever the job they do.

Are there any jobs in the media that Christians might feel they ought not to do to earn a living?

Does it matter if game shows encourage greed? Is there any harm in it?

Some Christians disagree with all gambling, whilst others see the lottery, football pools and bingo as harmless diversions, especially when some of the profits go to charity. What do you think?

On what things should Christians spend and not spend their money? Give reasons.

Many people spend a lot of money on the media.

All people, not just Christians, make decisions not only about how much money to spend on the media but how much time to give to it. The use of television is a good example to consider.

TELEVISION

On 27 January 1926 John Logie Baird gave the first public demonstration of his invention, the television.

FIND OUT

How many channels are available at present, including satellite and cable?

How much does it cost to subscribe to either a few sports channels or a few film channels?

How much time do you and your friends or family spend watching television in one week?

Many Christian families are concerned about the effect that television has on family life. Some see the TV set as being like a one-eyed idol, demanding attention and time. They feel that it has a bad effect on family life especially if families sit in front of it eating instead of making mealtimes a family occasion.

Few Christians refuse to own a television. Most Christians in the United Kingdom do use the media but they believe that they need to choose carefully what to watch and read. They may limit the time they spend and try not to neglect church attendance, for example, on Sundays.

Christian parents are likely to try to make sure that their children only watch programmes or read magazines that are suitable for their age group and which do not promote the wrong values. They are likely also to want to supervise their children when they use the internet.

FOR DISCUSSION

How far should any parents, not just Christian parents, control the money and time which their children spend on the media?

How far should parents control the content of what their children see and read?

INFLUENCE OF MEDIA ON LIFESTYLES

Wasting money and time is not the only media issue that might concern Christians. To some extent, popular culture is both created and reflected by the media. Some of the media present a view of the world that does not fit with Christian views about the priorities in life and the values people should live by. Lifestyles portrayed in the media and advertising may have a bad effect particularly on impressionable young people. In many drama series, for example, the main characters are married and divorced several times, have affairs and commit crimes. The stories are interesting and entertaining but they can give the impression that this is normal and acceptable behaviour.

FOR DISCUSSION

Some Christians would defend soap operas, saying that they serve a similar function to that of morality plays such as 'Everyman' in the Middle Ages. The stories help people to think about right and wrong and show them the possible consequences of their behaviour. What do you think?

ALCOHOL

The regular use of alcohol is another feature of many dramas. For some Christians this is one aspect of popular culture which goes against their ideals. Though they may enjoy a drink themselves sometimes, they are concerned at the emphasis on alcohol as essential to having a good time.

Christians belonging to some Protestant evangelical denominations are tee-total; they never drink alcohol. There are individual Christians in other traditions whose conscience may lead them also to abstain from it. Abstinence is not usually because these Christians are against pleasure. Mostly, it is because they have seen the harm that the consumption of excess alcohol can cause.

Other Christians believe that, for themselves, moderation is the key to living in the modern material world. They try to behave responsibly.

Many Christian denominations and individual believers feel they have to rethink how best to apply their principles as times change and society evolves. Methodism, for example, was associated with tee-totalism from its beginnings but in 1987 the Methodist Conference made this statement:

> All Methodists (should) consider seriously the claims of total abstinence, and make a personal commitment either to total abstinence or to responsible drinking.

The Bible does not condemn alcohol but it does condemn getting drunk.

> Do not join those who drink too much wine
> or gorge themselves on meat,
> for drunkards and gluttons become poor,
> and drowsiness clothes them in rags.
>
> (Proverbs 23:20–21)
>
> Do not gaze at wine when it is red,
> when it sparkles in the cup,
> when it goes down smoothly!
> In the end it bites like a snake
> and poisons like a viper.
> Your eyes will see strange sights
> and your mind imagine confusing things.
> You will be like one sleeping on the high seas,
> lying on top of the rigging.
> 'They hit me,' you will say, 'but I'm not hurt!
> They beat me, but I don't feel it!
> When will I wake up
> so I can find another drink?'
>
> (Proverbs 23:20–21, 31–35)

Wine was part of Israel's staple diet. To the present day the Jewish community treats alcohol as a gift from God. Every major Jewish religious festival is marked by the drinking of wine.

> He makes grass grow for the cattle,
> and plants for man to cultivate —
> bringing forth food from the earth:
> wine that gladdens the heart of man,
> oil to make his face shine,
> and bread that sustains his heart.   (Psalm 104:14–15)

According to the gospels, Jesus showed the same positive approach to alcohol. Jesus turned water into wine when he miraculously provided 600 litres at the wedding in Cana (John 2:1–10).

At the Last Supper, he commanded his disciples to break bread and drink wine in memory of him.

Paul advised Timothy to drink some wine:

> 'Stop drinking only water, and use a little wine because of your stomach and your frequent illnesses.'
>
> (1 Timothy 5:23)

It was Paul who recommended moderation in all things but it was also Paul who reminded the believers that, though their conscience might be clear, they should also consider the effect that their behaviour might have on other people.

> It is better not to eat meat or drink wine or to do anything else that will cause your brother to fall.
>
> (Romans 14:21)

The Christian Church uses Biblical teaching about alcohol to apply to the use and abuse of all drugs.

Christianity is not against pleasure but it is against selfishness. Selfish enjoyment is false pleasure according to the Christian viewpoint. Addicts become increasingly selfish and self-centred until they do not care whom they hurt.

Also, Christianity is against all forms of addiction because addicts have placed something other than God at the centre of their lives and lifestyles.

Sometimes in their attempts to do good, Christians have restricted the freedom of other people. Prohibition in America is often given as an example of this approach. In America in 1920 the manufacture, transport and sale of alcoholic beverages were totally banned. As a result of banning alcohol, it is said that:

- people drank more, not less
- ordinary people began to show disrespect for the law
- criminal activity increased.

Prohibition in America ended in 1933.

ROLE MODELS

Another way the media influences lifestyles is by creating role models. In the West, we live in a consumer society. People buy things to fit the lifestyle they want. Fame is big business. Film stars, pop stars and sports celebrities fill the media in the western world and it is very difficult, in particular for young people, to ignore the role models of popular culture.

Christians feel that the media tends to make idols of people. For some, this is breaking the second commandment which tells them not to make idols nor worship false images.

What good will it be for a man if he gains the whole world, yet forfeits his soul? Or what can a man give in exchange for his soul? (Matthew 16:26)

The New Testament attitude to fame is expressed in this verse.

As larger numbers of television and radio channels compete to fill their schedules with cheaper and cheaper material, the 'reality TV' programmes, live talk shows and talent-spotting contests flood the networks. The message is that anybody can become a star. The word 'wannabee' is now included in dictionaries.

People sometimes criticise programmes because they are considered to be in poor taste, crude, coarse or vulgar. The word vulgar comes from the Latin for 'the common people'. Christianity set out to be a religion for the common people. Some light entertainment programmes may be brash in style but they can be helpful to viewers in coping with everyday life. They show how to get on with other people and give insights into the way various individuals think. It is important to distinguish the aims and content of a programme from the style of presentation.

MUSIC

The popular music scene has a great influence on young people. In shops, music is used to control people's mood. It is part of merchandising. The purpose is to encourage the public to happily buy more goods.

One of the reasons the early Christian Church chose to celebrate Christmas in December was that they hoped to clamp down on rowdy winter celebrations and replace them with a more solemn ceremony. Saint Augustine (b.354 CE) declared, 'If they must have songs, let them sing the music of the church.'

In the present day, most secular popular music continues to be about love and all the sentiments that go with finding love and losing love. Some Christians feel that popular songs trivialise relationships, are too obsessed with sex and may lead to lustful thoughts and bad behaviour.

Individuals may find their own sense of identity when they recognise others who share their taste in music. Songs can unite protesters and give them a sense of solidarity. Music can be the sound of rebellion and might be used to undermine established authority.

Attitudes towards music and popular culture have relaxed among many Christian denominations over the years. Churches use popular musical forms and styles in worship. Most Christians listen to pop music just like anybody else and many Christians work in the pop music industry and in other areas of the performing arts.

OTHER INFLUENCES

Some Christians feel that another important issue for all religions concerning the influence of the media is the popularising of New Age ideas. Ever since the hippies of the 1960s, popular culture and the media have retained a nostalgia for flower power ideas. Many people share the concern for peace, love, nature and the environment. There is wide interest in spirituality, mysticism, meditation and alternative holistic approaches to medicine and lifestyles. Some religious people, however, fear that the articles and programmes may give confusing or misleading ideas.

Astrology is big business and features in most newspapers. Despite the wise men following the star, Christians tend to think that basing your life on any sort of fortune telling is silly or wrong. Most Christians are uneasy about media themes which they think may lead impressionable people to dabble in the occult.

FOR DISCUSSION

Some Christians are concerned about the popularity of Star Wars, Lord of the Rings, Harry Potter, the Narnia books and other fantasy worlds.

Should children be encouraged to believe in magic?

Do battles between good and evil contradict Christian teaching?

Should Christians only read and watch non-fiction?

ADVERTISING

It is not only the articles and the programmes in the media which influence people. The adverts also affect people's attitudes. We are told that we will be happier, more successful, sexier or healthier if we buy a particular product and this might be anything from a fizzy drink to furniture or a new car. Psychologists and market researchers help advertisers to target various groups of people in society. Peer pressure then helps to promote the product as a desirable article.

Advertising can encourage people to be greedy and to consume more than they really need. It can emphasise the differences between rich and poor and make people feel inadequate, envious and resentful.

Many people, not only Christians, feel that advertising promotes the wrong kind of values. It is part of a consumer society in which people judge others by what they own rather than what they are. Advertising encourages people to covet. This is against the tenth commandment. Even children are targeted and parents feel under pressure to provide the latest trendy gear and feel guilty if they cannot afford it.

Despite all the concerns about the manipulation of the public by advertising, it is accepted as an inevitable feature of modern life. Churches and charities advertise their events just like anybody else. Advertising serves a valuable function in telling the public what is available or what is new.

FOR DISCUSSION

Should Christians work in advertising? Give reasons and consider other points of view.

There is a famous prayer made popular by American theologian Dr Reinhold Niebuhr in the 1930s as the serenity prayer. It reads:

God grant me the serenity to accept the things I cannot change, the courage to change the things I can and the wisdom to know the difference.

An advertisement for a building society has taken this over. How do you think Christians might and should react?

Very few people want to ban advertising and the media totally but there are many religious groups including some Christians who petition the government or local authorities when they feel that a poster, an article, a book, a play or a film are offensive. Pressure groups try to influence the situation so that what has offended them is banned or censored.

FOR DISCUSSION

Which is the most recent incident you can think of in the news where a poster, book, film, play, programme or a celebrity of screen, music or sport has upset people of any religion?

CENSORSHIP

In most countries, there are laws of obscenity. Some countries, like Ireland and Italy, are stricter than others. The same applies to some states in America.

The word 'obscene' is used to describe material which is likely to deprave and corrupt the public. In the United Kingdom, when the publishers of *Lady Chatterley's Lover* were acquitted of obscenity in 1960, it started a gradual process of society becoming more broadminded. Prosecutions for obscenity today are mainly confined to the display of photographs and graphics. The offence depends on the effect on the audience or readership.

Censorship usually involves someone in authority deciding what other people can read or see. The word comes from the job of the censor, which existed in ancient Rome from 443–22 BCE.

Censorship can be a difficult issue. On the one hand people want to protect the vulnerable members of society. They fear, for example, that young children may be influenced to copy bad things they have seen. On the other hand there is the danger of eroding people's individual freedom. Freedom of speech and freedom of the press are important means of making sure that countries do not become dictatorships or police states.

In the United Kingdom, some people campaign against sex and violence in the media, especially on television, and the watershed is a sort of compromise.

The watershed – nine o'clock at night – marks the time after which more explicit material can be shown on television.

SEX AND VIOLENCE

Gratuitous sex and violence means using sex and violence which is not necessary for the plot but which will attract a bigger audience. Nowadays, especially in the western world, people are more liberal minded than in the past and they happily watch scenes which might have shocked previous generations.

In the New Testament Paul says:

> Finally, brothers, whatever is true, whatever is noble, whatever is right, whatever is pure, whatever is lovely, whatever is admirable – if anything is excellent or praiseworthy – think about such things.
>
> (Philippians 4:8)

Many Christians are concerned about the frequency, scale and explicitness of violence and sex in the media.

VIOLENCE

Some Christians are pacifists but on the whole Christianity is not a pacifist religion. Even in a situation of war, the aim is ultimately to establish peace and Christians are not supposed to encourage or condone cruelty in any situation.

Some films seem to glorify war and scenes of destruction and violent action can easily be justified as essential to a plot of a story-line.

On television, however, news programmes report on the violence in the world every day. The newsreels are censored by the television companies themselves so that viewers are not too distressed by what they see but wars, terrorism and violence have to be reported if they are part of the day's news. The documentaries and films which have anti-war themes still bring the subject into people's homes.

Some people feel that the media encourages violence and other people disagree but there is another important issue. There is the danger that frequent exposure to violence in the media results in the public becoming desensitised. The public begins to accept that the world has always been a violent place and is no longer shocked by the physical or verbal abuse of vulnerable members of society.

SEX

Christian Churches generally teach that sex outside marriage is wrong. In the past, most people would have agreed with them. Society was much more strict about sex mainly because people were afraid of some of the consequences such as sexually transmitted diseases and unwanted pregnancies. There was a great deal of stigma and shame associated with anyone in a family 'getting into trouble' or being 'illegitimate'. The media often points out in dramas and documentaries that guilt and hypocrisy caused much unhappiness when people repressed their sexual feelings.

Christians may have differing attitudes towards what is acceptable in relationships and sexual behaviour. Christian Churches that take literally the New Testament teachings still hold traditional views about sexual prohibitions. They are likely to condemn the media for any material which seems to condone promiscuity, pre-marital sex, adultery and homosexuality. However, all Christians would agree on some fundamental beliefs which are relevant when discussing sex in the media. Christians believe that each person is made in the image of God so each human being is unique and special. Every individual should be treated with respect. Christians also believe that sex is a gift from God and should be part of a loving relationship.

Love is patient, love is kind. It does not envy, it does not boast, it is not proud. It is not rude, it is not self-seeking, it is not easily angered, it keeps no record of wrongs. Love does not delight in evil but rejoices with the truth. It always protects, always trusts, always hopes, always perseveres. Love never fails. But where there are prophecies, they will cease; where there are tongues, they will be stilled; where there is knowledge, it will pass away.

(1 Corinthians 13:4–8)

PORNOGRAPHY

Pornography is the explicit description or showing of sexual activity. The term comes from the Greek words for prostitute and writing and originally referred to works of art and writing describing the life of prostitutes.

Though pornography is wrong in the opinion of some people, not only Christians, changing social attitudes now mean that it is no longer a criminal offence in most western countries.

In the United Kingdom and the USA some citizens (religious and secular) have asked their governments to restrict the availability of offensive material on the internet.

FOR DISCUSSION

What would you like to censor in the media, if anything?

Is censorship a good or a bad thing? Give reasons.

CENSORSHIP IN CHRISTIANITY

The term 'Big Brother' was used in the book *1984* by George Orwell. It was published in 1949 but was set in a fictional nightmare future where there was total invasion of privacy. Everywhere there were posters with pictures of the leader of the party in power. The slogan was, 'Big Brother is watching you'. There was a two-way television screen in every room and the state tried to have complete control even of people's thoughts. Words like Newspeak and Doublethink were used by the author to show that the state had absolute power over all media. Newspeak was where language was used to hide the truth from people.

One of the reasons that people in the western world are suspicious of censorship is because they remember past history, particularly the Nazi propaganda in the 1930s and the censorship in communist countries such as the former Union of Soviet Republics where atheism was the established view and there was a one-party state.

When thinking about Christian views on issues of censorship, it is important to distinguish between crimes and sins. Crimes break the laws of the state. Sins break commands which people believe came from God. Some actions, like murder, are both a sin and a crime.

In the United Kingdom in the 1960s, a committee under the chairmanship of Lord Wolfenden considered how far it was acceptable for a society to pass laws governing moral behaviour. It concluded that, unless we were to say that there is no difference between a crime and a sin, there must remain an area of our private lives that is 'quite simply not the Law's business'.

The most dramatic censorship of written material is when books are burnt. Burning of books has become a symbol of a repressive society. In two thousand years of Christian history the Church has had a great deal of experience of censorship. Sometimes Christians have been the victims and sometimes they have been the ones suppressing the opinions and books of others.

In Acts 19:19, Paul's converts at Ephesus burnt their books of sorcery. This is sometimes used as the first example of Christian censorship but in this situation the books belonged to the people who burnt them. They were repenting their past and wanted to make a fresh start.

The Roman emperor Constantine decreed toleration of Christianity. Less than 20 years later, Constantine ordered the burning of the books of the Greek theologian Arius. The aim was to suppress heresy.

Theodosius I became emperor in 392 BCE and made Christianity the established religion of the Empire. The Roman government and the Church began to persecute both pagans and Christian heretics. Books that expressed ideas of faith and morals contrary to official Church teaching were prohibited and authors punished. The stated purpose was to try to give stability to society in very troubled times.

The first catalogue of forbidden books was issued by Pope Gelasius in 496 BCE.

Pope Gregory IX instituted the Inquisition in 1231 for the purpose of enforcing religious censorship.

In the fifteenth century, the invention of printing spread ideas rapidly but censorship soon regained control. Pope Innocent VIII introduced pre-publication censorship in 1487 and in 1559 Pope Paul first issued the Index of Forbidden Books.

In England, Henry VIII became head of the Church of England, instead of the Pope, and the Act of Supremacy 1534 gave him the power to declare and punish heresies. He persecuted papists and reformers and burnt copies of the English translation of the New Testament. Printers had to submit all manuscripts to Church authorities before publication.

Despite government restrictions, people like John Wycliffe and William Tyndale translated the Bible into English. Tyndale was executed in 1536.

Eventually, in the reign of King James I, the Authorised Version of the Bible was printed in 1611 in English. People could read the Bible for themselves. This helped to encourage the founding of non-conformist denominations. The Church of England was part of the State so non-conformity was seen as treason.

Oliver Cromwell in the seventeenth century established a licensing system for books and newspapers and there was censorship of anything 'contrary to good life and manners'. It was abolished in 1695.

Historians regard the eighteenth century as the beginning of the modern period in the western world. There was an emphasis on toleration and liberty that reflected the influence of the Age of Enlightenment, the American War of Independence and the French Revolution. People were tired of centuries of religious conflict and intolerance. Freedom of speech and freedom of the press were seen as important if people were to exercise their right to bring about peaceful changes in government.

Some Christians still turn to their own particular Church leaders to be guided in what books and pamphlets to read. The last edition of the Roman Catholic Index of Forbidden books was issued in 1948. It was discontinued in the 1960s though the Church may still give recommendations about reading matter.

is not appropriate to have acts of worship, unless all world faiths are represented.

THE RELATIONSHIP OF CHRISTIANITY TO THE MEDIA AND THE USE OF THE MEDIA BY CHRISTIANITY

In the United Kingdom, television and radio have always had an important role in bringing religious programmes and issues to the public. When the BBC started regular television broadcasting in 1946 it concentrated on religious programmes on Sundays between 10.30 a.m. and 12 noon and from 6.00 p.m. until 7 p.m. (2½ hours). These times became known as the 'God Slot' and were almost always entirely of Christian content, mostly Protestant denominations and particularly involving the Church of England. Acts of worship with hymns and sermons were broadcast on radio and television in the Sunday God-slots. Programmes were seen as providing an opportunity for those who were housebound to join in acts of worship.

Many Christians believe that religion is part of everyday life and they did not want religion pushed aside into a God-slot. There were others who wanted the God-slot as an opportunity to convert people. These are still topics for debate but other issues have arisen. Some people feel that in a pluralist society it

As the United Kingdom became more of a pluralist society, broadcasting tried to reflect the changes in society. The BBC had always taken seriously the responsibility to educate. Educational TV and radio have covered multifaith issues for many years. Nowadays the BBC and commercial stations have regular discussion programmes in popular time-slots on religious ethics and documentaries on the specific beliefs and practices of various world faiths. People of minority faiths in the United Kingdom feel this will lessen prejudice and encourage more considerate treatment during religious fasts and festivals, as well as give outsiders the opportunity to find out more about the religion.

Most Christians in the United Kingdom increasingly accept the importance of inter-faith dialogue and so do the media. On most official public occasions and at times of national crisis, the media broadcast speeches from leaders of the main faiths represented in the country.

The media and the public in the United Kingdom have mixed attitudes about the relevance of traditional institutions in the modern world. A good example is the debate about the value of the monarchy and the Royal family. Some people would like the United Kingdom to be a republic and to have a president instead of a king or queen. Pageantry, pomp and ceremony give a country a sense of identity. Christianity is part of the history, culture and heritage of the United Kingdom. The Anglican tradition has been the established Church in England for nearly five hundred years with the ruling monarch as the head of the Church of England. Prince Charles has said, however, that he would prefer the title for the monarchy to be 'defender of the faiths' not simply of Christianity.

In some ways the Anglican Church has been in a privileged position but in other ways it can be a disadvantage when Church and state are tied together. Disestablishment of the Church is discussed by Christians as well as by the rest of society.

One of the issues in the United Kingdom has been the matter of laws against blasphemy. Blasphemy consists of offensive or abusive remarks about God.

In the 1970s (the case of *Lemon v. Gay News*) the newspaper *Gay News* published an illustration and a poem by American writer James Kirkup which suggested that Jesus might have been homosexual. The court case established that there was a crime of blasphemy in common law and the editor of *Gay*

News was prosecuted. In the 1980s, when Salman Rushdie wrote *The Satanic Verses*, which caused offence to many Muslims, the courts decided that, in England, blasphemy offered protection only to Christianity and possibly only to the Church of England.

Many people, not only Muslims, felt that the situation was unfair. They thought the blasphemy law should apply to all faiths or none. To extend the law on blasphemy could seriously curtail the right to freedom of speech.

FOR DISCUSSION

It is said that all publicity is good publicity. In what situations do you think reporting on famous people is invasion of privacy?

When is passing on news just gossip?

How far do you think the public have a right to know everything?

PREJUDICE AND DISCRIMINATION IN THE MEDIA

Prejudice means having an attitude, a pre-judged opinion, which is biased and not based on facts. Discrimination means the ability to distinguish between things. It has also come to mean an action which treats people unfairly on the basis of prejudice.

The media has been criticised for the part it plays in perpetuating stereotypes. For example, some people now see the role of housewife in plays and advertisements as a sex-stereotype just as degrading as the images of women as pin-ups.

Stereotypes are based on and encourage prejudiced opinions. They lead to people being thought of and treated as types rather than individuals. In the past there have been stereotypes in comedy programmes which modern viewers would perceive as racist. Viewers are more educated nowadays, more aware of prejudiced attitudes and more willing to complain.

In Britain, the Race Relations Act 1976 makes it unlawful to discriminate against anyone on the grounds of race, colour, nationality or ethnic origin. It gives people the right to claim compensation for discrimination, harassment and victimisation. It applies to jobs, training, housing, education and the provisions of goods, facilities and services. Racial violence and other racial incidents are offences under criminal law. Inciting racial hatred is also a criminal offence. However, racial prejudice cannot be made illegal because it is an attitude not an action. Laws cannot be made to censor people's thoughts.

All religions in the United Kingdom support government legislation which tries to make a fairer society where the rights of individuals are protected.

Most Christians are aware of the past history of Christianity and have had to face some unpleasant truths about the prejudice and bigotry between various groups of Christians but also about the involvement of Christianity in slavery, apartheid, racism and colonialism. They are also aware that similar atrocities continue today. In the past and now, there have been individual Christians and Churches that have tried to change injustices in society. There are many Christians therefore who object to the stereotyping of Christianity in the media, just as much as they dislike stereotypes of any other people.

FOR DISCUSSION

How biased do you think the media is about religion? If you don't know, find out. Keep a record of articles in the press. Watch for any type of bias.

Humour is a very difficult issue in the media. Do you think people should never be allowed to make fun of religion?

The difficulty for comedy programmes is the fact that humour often relies on stereotypes. Writers are cautious of making fun of minority faiths so Christianity gets the brunt of such humour. Stereotypes often do contain a grain of truth or they would not exist in the first place.

Many Christians treat humour in the media as harmless, depending on the intention of the writers, even when cartoons portray caricatures of Christians.

One distinction that needs to be considered when studying religion and the media is the difference between education and propaganda.

Education is usually thought to be a good thing. Propaganda, on the other hand, is thought to be misleading. The trouble is that one person's idea of education might be seen by another person as propaganda.

Education is supposed to try to present various sides of an issue so people can make an informed decision. Reasons for doubting something as well as grounds for believing should be considered. Skills are taught so that students can learn to find relevant data, understand the significance of the information and evaluate various views about an issue. Propaganda uses selected facts, arguments, rumours, half-truths and lies to distort information. The aim is to influence public opinion but it appeals to prejudice and irrational emotions.

Increasingly TV evangelism is seen by satellite and cable. Often these are American programmes, almost all made by Christians. Some of the presenters are known as televangelists or the electronic preachers. Their organisations can be worth millions of dollars.

Until the 1980s television companies in the United States had to give some free air time to religious institutions. Now religious programmes have to be paid for and broadcasts are expensive. Religious broadcasters beg for money, some of which is spent buying more airtime. The media itself has reported scandals involving the lifestyles of some evangelists and the use of the money raised.

The United Kingdom has people of many faiths and it has usually been understood by the media that their purpose is not to convert people to any particular religion. It remains an issue for discussion especially since more and more TV channels are becoming available and the electronic revolution spreads further every day.

American Evangelist Billy Graham once said, 'In a single telecast I preach to millions more than Christ did in his lifetime.'

Christianity is a missionary faith. From the beginning Jesus urged his followers to communicate the gospel, the good news. The Greek word for good news is 'euanggelion'. We get the word evangelist from this. The first Christians spread the message and taught the converts using the media of the time. The gospels and the epistles were part of this process.

There is a transcript of a trial of some Christians who were executed in North Africa in 180 CE. The Roman magistrate asks what the scrolls are that the Christian men and women have with them in a box. He is told that they are 'copies of letters from a just man called Paul'. Eventually the books and letters preserved by the Christians were collected into the New Testament.

Then the invention of printing made mass media possible.

As a result of centuries of Christian missionary work, Bibles are available now in more than 300 languages, complete New Testaments in approximately 700 and some chapters in a further thousand. Sometimes this has involved putting a language in writing for the very first time. Translating, printing and distributing Bibles, at times illegally in some countries, has played a big part in Christian history (see Chapter 7).

In 2002, Zondervann Books published the New Testament translation as part of Today's New International Version of the Bible. It is politically correct in that it is gender neutral and avoids the use of terms like 'all men' to refer to people in general. The conservative Southern Baptist churches and other evangelicals in 'the Bible Belt' were deeply offended by this break with tradition.

ICT FOR RESEARCH

For Zondervann: www.tniv.info/bible/index.php

For other Bibles: www.biblegateway.com

Compare John 11:25

Jesus said to her, 'I am the resurrection and the life. He who believes in me will live, even though he dies'.

EDUCATION

Teaching people to read has been and still is a priority with many Christians. Schools have been established by most Christian denominations in various countries around the world.

Education in the United Kingdom owes a great deal to the efforts of various Churches over the centuries.

The Education Act of 1944 sorted out the educational system in England and Wales. Similar reforms were made soon afterwards for Scotland and Northern Ireland. The government recognised the pioneering work of voluntary bodies like Churches in providing education in the past so they retained the existing schools in the system. Today there are about seven thousand 'Church schools' as part of the state system in Britain including some Jewish and

Methodist schools. The first British state-funded Islamic schools were established in 1998. Privately run schools now exist in the United Kingdom to cater for Christians, Muslims, Sikhs and Orthodox Jews.

Serious issues have been raised by the media about faith schools in the United Kingdom, for example, some people believe that faith schools can be racially divisive. Some other issues concern the curriculum. There are fears of indoctrination and that the education might be biased towards religious dogma.

FOR DISCUSSION

One debate is whether literal creationism should be allowed to be taught as a valid alternative to scientific evolutionary theory. What do you think?

The 1944 Education Act required that, in every state primary and secondary school, the day should begin with an act of collective worship and that there should be some religious instruction. This was partly because the government was worried about moral standards in society after the Second World War but also because they felt that education needed some input for all aspects of a human being – body, mind and spirit. The law included a conscience clause to protect individual pupils and teachers from having to attend lessons or assemblies if it was against their beliefs.

These lessons were known by names such as Religious Knowledge, Bible Study, Scripture or Divinity. Gradually the name for the subject changed as lessons moved away from biblical studies to include world faiths and contemporary moral and ethical issues.

In 1988 the Education Reform Act left Religious Education as compulsory. Religion adds an extra dimension to living and many people see it as an important part of education, especially in a multicultural society. There are some Christians, however, and some members of other faiths, who are uncomfortable with the idea of Religious Education and do not think it should be compulsory in state schools.

THE ATTITUDES OF CHRISTIANS TO THE USE OF THE MEDIA TO PRESENT THE CHRISTIAN MESSAGE

Throughout history Christians have used all types of media.

ICT FOR RESEARCH

Look up ideas for wayside pulpits under 'posters' at www.churchsupplies.org.uk

MUSIC

Jesus and his disciples sang a hymn at the Last Supper before they set out for the Mount of Olives. Paul in his letters encouraged the singing of 'psalms, hymns and spiritual songs with gratitude in your hearts to God' (Colossians 3:16).

The early Christians used to sing psalms like the Jews did in the synagogue.

The liturgy, rituals and symbols of Orthodox worship developed differently from those in the West. The Orthodox Church still have chanting because they feel that musical instruments interfere between the worshipper and God.

In the West, some Christian services have very elaborate formal ceremonies of music and choral singing. Many classical composers have written religious music for church use, such as Mozart's Requiem and Bach's St Matthew Passion.

The words of most church music were in Latin for centuries. In 129 CE Telesphorus, the eighth pope, announced that the angels' hymn 'Gloria in Excelsis' heard by the shepherds should be sung during Christmas services.

Saint Francis of Assisi was one of the first to use popular country tunes and everyday language so that local peasants could join in Christmas celebrations. He even arranged to have some villagers acting the story in a stable in the village of Greccio in 1223.

Music, besides being part of worship, is a powerful means of popularising Christian ideas. Charles Wesley (1707–88) wrote over 450 Methodist hymns such as 'Love divine, all loves excelling' and 'Jesu, lover of my soul'. George Frideric Handel, wrote music for some of Wesley's hymns but, of course, is best known for his own great work, Handel's *Messiah*.

General William Booth (1829–1912) the founder of the Salvation Army said, 'Why should the devil have all the good tunes?' He had no reservations about using brass band musical instruments.

The St Thomas More centre in London was founded in 1969 as a bookshop, conference centre and place where new Roman Catholic music could be published.

Mahalia Jackson, the 'Queen of Gospel' (1911–72), sang at the inauguration of President Kennedy.

This verse was the inspiration for Pentecostal praise:

> *Let everything that breathes praise the LORD!*
>
> (Psalm 150:6)

The Bible is full of song lyrics. This song was sung by Jewish Exiles, captured in war and forced to live away from home:

> *By the rivers of Babylon we sat and wept*
> *when we remembered Zion.*
> *There on the poplars*
> *we hung our harps,*
> *for there our captors asked us for songs,*
> *our tormentors demanded songs of joy;*
> *they said, 'Sing us one of the songs of Zion!'*
> *How can we sing the songs of the Lord*
> *while in a foreign land?*
> *If I forget you, O Jerusalem,*
> *may my right hand forget its skill.*
> *May my tongue cling to the roof of my mouth*
> *if I do not remember you,*
> *if I do not consider Jerusalem*
> *my highest joy.*
>
> (Psalm 137:1–6)

The London-based Prom Praise are led by the orchestra of All Souls Langham Place, a church which is a centre for Christian Arts.

New hymns and chants from all denominations cross the boundaries of denominations freely.

Most Christian Churches have hymn books which they use in worship.

All styles of music have found their way into Christianity. Sometimes it has worked the other way round also. Gospel music of the Pentecostal Churches in America had a big effect on popular music styles.

Bunyan in Prison.

FOR DISCUSSION

'Music is the most spiritual of all modes of expression.'
William Temple, Archbishop of Canterbury 1942–44.
Do you agree?

When does worship become a concert?

ICT FOR RESEARCH

Who are the modern hymn writers? Look in *Mission Praise* (1983), *Songs of Fellowship* (1985) or in a school hymn book.

This postcard reached Terry Waite and gave him hope during his imprisonment. As the Special Envoy of the Archbishop of Canterbury, Terry Waite was trying to negotiate the release of hostages in the Lebanon in 1987 when he himself was taken by terrorists. He was in captivity for nearly five years.

Graham Kendrick has written some of the most popular modern hymns and songs.

Psalms need not be sung, they can also be read as poetry. Many poets and writers who explored mystical and metaphysical ideas were brought up as devout Christians. Some also wrote hymns.

EXPRESSING CHRISTIAN BELIEFS IN ART AND DRAMA

For many faiths the presentation of religious figures and stories causes some problems but often the dramatisation or drawing of cartoons is thought to help children in particular to learn about the history and stories of a religion. Visual images can be helpful in catching people's interest. Some Christians prefer simplicity in their worship and

surroundings so as not to distract the soul from communication with God but even the Society of Friends, the Quakers, have a drama group called the Leaveners that runs workshops for young people interested in drama.

ICT FOR RESEARCH

Greenbelt started in 1973 as a small pop festival run by Christians. About 1,500 young people turned up. Now the pop and arts festival caters for all age groups, takes over the Cheltenham racecourse for a week and is sponsored by organisations such as Christian Aid and YMCA. Find out the line-up for this year on the Greenbelt website.

www.greenbelt.org.uk

Americans Carol and Jimmy Owens have written Christian musicals and, in the United Kingdom, Roger Jones, originally a teacher in Birmingham, devises Christian entertainments which are musicals for church use. The models for these sorts of musicals come from the secular music industry, particularly the work of Tim Rice and Andrew Lloyd Webber. 'Joseph and the Amazing Technicolor Dreamcoat' (1968) and the rock opera 'Jesus Christ Superstar' (1970) had enormous impact as did the American musical 'Godspell'.

Many Christians were shocked by rock musicals on biblical themes but most Christians and churches who are not against using the media have accepted these musical shows.

There have been and always will be some religious people who disapprove of the theatrical world. The reason may be simply because acting is pretence or they might think actors lead decadent lives.

Religious people sometimes feel uncomfortable at the representation of important religious figures in drama. For example, some Christians think that God or Jesus should not be impersonated.

Some Christians are not only against the representation of important religious people but also of any person and all living creatures. This view is based on the first two commandments given by God

to the prophet Moses. The first commandment is about not having other gods besides the one God. The second commandment says:

> *You shall not make for yourself an idol in the form of anything in heaven above or on the earth beneath or in the waters below. You shall not bow down to them or worship them . . .*   (Exodus 20:4–5a)

Some Christian churches do have statues and paintings whilst some do not.

Christians who use icons, statues and paintings in their churches are not ignoring the second commandment. To them, religious art is an aid to the worship of the one God. The command is not against making things but against making an idol, something to be worshipped.

Christians who do not have statues in places of worship want to make sure that there is not any possibility of treating statues and pictures as idols. To make an image of any living thing is disobedience to the command in their view. It is also insulting to the Creator God to try to create a copy of something God made. Many Protestant Churches today continue to be simple and plain in design but happily incorporate artworks and paintings to express their beliefs.

It seems clear looking back at history that the Roman Catholic and Eastern Orthodox Churches never saw religious art nor religious drama as a problem.

In Europe in the Middle Ages, few people could read and plays and stained glass windows helped them to learn Bible stories. Dramatisation of sacred stories was common.

Mystery plays, miracle plays and morality plays were used for entertainment in both religious and secular life as appropriate to the situation. During religious festivals, parts of the Bible story were acted in different corners of the local church or in some nearby convenient location. Some were very pious performances but many of these plays had lots of coarse language and jokes. In nativity plays the shepherds were comic characters and Herod was booed as the villain. Plays were sometimes performed on carts, pageant wagons, and were more like what we might expect in pantomime.

ICT FOR RESEARCH

Find out about the fourteenth-century cycle of 25 scriptural plays, or mystery plays, performed at Chester. Some other surviving cycles are those of York and Wakefield.

In the United Kingdom, Victorian paintings of Jesus and illustrations in children's Bibles showed Jesus as blonde and blue eyed. Today such paintings are considered unacceptable by many Christians. They are inaccurate because Jesus was Jewish and the pictures are a reminder of the association of British missionaries in the past with colonial rule. In fact, however, Christians around the world have painted pictures of Jesus throughout Christian history in a variety of different ways to express their beliefs about him. Often they wanted to link Jesus with their own cultures and causes.

Obviously there are no photographs of Jesus Christ. The first images of Jesus which still exist are from the third century and were found in the catacombs in Rome. Fifth-century mosaics at Ravenna look more like Apollo and show Jesus as a clean-shaven young man.

ICT FOR RESEARCH

Look in Encarta for 'Pantocrator' to see Christian Byzantine Art and Christ as Pantocrator which means the ruler of everything. From the sixth century this was the usual way the face of Jesus Christ looked in icons in the Orthodox Church. The face was based on the Mandylion ('holy face'). The holy face was on a cloth which was revered in the early Church. The image itself was called the Saviour Acheiropoietos (image 'not made by man' Mark 14:58). The cloth was called the Veronika (meaning true image) and there were legends about how the face came to be on the cloth. One story was that Saint Veronica mopped the sweat from the face of Jesus as he carried his cross to Calvary and by a miracle the image came on to the cloth.

Pictures and paintings are another way of telling a story.

Every brushstroke of an icon is said to have been accompanied by a prayer. This makes the picture holy and Orthodox Christians believe that when they touch an icon they receive blessings from God who inspired the painting.

ICT FOR RESEARCH

Many of the world's greatest artists have painted religious pictures based on Christianity. Look up Michelangelo in Encarta and see the Sistine Chapel.

Religious art is often rich in symbolism. Mary, the mother of Jesus, has a special place in the hearts and minds of Christians. Symbols like the lily and the blue robe indicate her purity (see Chapter 1).

In England in the civil war the Roundheads and Puritans smashed stained glass windows because they wanted to cleanse the churches of idolatrous images. They thought that the Christian Church had grown corrupt and was full of superstition. They knocked the heads off statues and carvings. The word iconoclast means a person who breaks religious statues and we also use it for someone who demolishes established ideas.

The Roundheads were not the first people to smash images because of religious zeal. Art and religion in the Byzantine Empire were disrupted by iconoclasm between 726 and 843 CE. Some Christians felt that the expression of spirituality in art looked like idolatry, especially the mosaics and icons showing devotion to the Virgin Mary as Theotokos. This is the Greek for 'God bearer' and describes Mary in her role as mother of God.

Some Christians used the existence of the mandylion to show that Jesus could not have been against reverence for sacred images. A theologian called St John of Damascus (675–749 CE) defended the use of icons as pictorial language. He compared them with the theological language of the gospels. Eventually Byzantine art was restored but an important distinction had been made about the use of icons. It was established that venerating icons is not the same as worshipping icons. Veneration means to show reverence and to treat with respectful devotion.

If attitudes to paintings and statues have caused so much controversy in the past, it is no wonder that there are differing opinions among Christians about the use of modern media. Some Christians continue

ICT FOR RESEARCH

Find an icon of St John of Damascus.

www.goarch.org/access/resources/clipart

to be cautious about showing a representation of religious figures, especially Jesus, on the screen.

Films and books tend to add or omit parts of any story. Editing is necessary to make sense of the whole or to fit into a time slot so any portrayal automatically becomes an interpretation. It can never be the whole truth.

Despite popular distrust of reporters and photojournalists, there are many people working in

Do you feel that such films are disrespectful?

the media who try to be objective and truthful. The problem with media is that every medium can be used to communicate lies. It is said that the camera does not lie but by choosing to print one picture as opposed to another, an interpretation has been given.

POLITICAL AND COMMERCIAL INTERESTS; THE CONTROL OF THE MEDIA

Nobody doubts that mass media and information industries have enormous power over people. But who has power over the media?

Political and commercial interests control much of the world. The influence of huge multinational companies is felt in the media. The extent to which they control the media, in various countries and globally, continues to be a matter of opinion and debate.

An example of political power is the use of D-notices in the United Kingdom. D-notices may be invoked to restrict the publication of information relating to matters of national security, for example in times of war. The government alert the press about events which may have a security risk but request that the information remains unpublished.

It is no coincidence in civil wars and political coups that the rebels try to seize the control of the media as soon as possible.

In the United Kingdom, like in most countries, the press are allowed to give their political views and support a particular party. The BBC public service is financially supported to a large extent by the money that the public pay in television licences. The BBC is supposed to be impartial and tries to give a balanced point of view about politics.

Politics and commercial interests cannot be easily separated. Silvio Berlusconi, the most powerful person in the Italian media, became Prime Minister of Italy. The terms media mogul, media magnate and media baron are used of people who own media empires.

Christianity has no united policy about the media. For example, there are some Christian sects such as Amish Mennonites and Exclusive Plymouth Brethren that condemn virtually every form of secular entertainment and there are, at the other extreme, individual Christians among the media barons who build up empires in the press.

There are many people including Christians of all persuasions who are concerned about media issues. In the European Community there is a limit on the percentage of non-European material which can be shown on the main television channels. This is intended to protect the European culture and lifestyles from American and Japanese influence.

Some people worry about the influence on attitudes and lifestyles whilst others are concerned also about ethical principles raised by the increasing use of information technology.

Being able to access information is not necessarily a good thing if the facts are incorrect or biased.

The Bible makes a distinction between knowledge and wisdom. Knowing lots of facts, even if they are all accurate, may not make people wise.

> *Many will go here and there to increase knowledge.*
> (Daniel 12:4)

This is a description of the futility of the pursuit of knowledge at the end of time.

An important issue is access to the media. The freedom to express one's views and the right of the public to receive information both depend on people having access to the media.

The world is divided into the information rich and the information poor. The developing countries are worried about the control of most of the world's media by the West. Meanwhile, within each country the division between the information rich and the information poor is getting wider also.

For many Christians this is a matter of principle. It is part of liberation theology. The gospel is 'the good news to the poor'. That is why the issues concerning the media are so important. It is not simply so Christians can preach to the world. The issue is that if everybody becomes information rich but the media is in the hands of big business interests, dictators or corrupt politicians then world problems are likely to become worse. Communication is supposed to build communities. People are meant to be able to join in. It is participatory. Developments in interactive technology in video, desktop publishing, mobile phones and computer networks have the potential to empower ordinary people.

The media in its many forms is part of our lives whether we like what it presents to us or not. The majority of Christians realise that we cannot ignore it nor the issues concerning the media and mass communication.

The first international congress of the World Association for Christian Communication was held in Manila in 1989 to identify and discuss media issues.

ICT FOR RESEARCH

Find out which Christian Churches belong to the World Association of Christian Communication.

www.wacc.org.uk.

FOR DISCUSSION

Sometimes it takes only one photographic image to imprint an event on people's minds, or to stir the world's conscience. One book or one song may become the shared symbol of an era or of a protest movement. Can you think of examples of this phenomenon?

Media can be the voice of the people and unite world efforts to solve global problems. Churches and individual Christians join in with those of other persuasions to support charities such as Comic Relief and media popstar campaigns, for example to feed the world.

Some Christians work in or run charities. Increasingly, Churches and charities use media experts to run their campaigns. Most Christians feel that it is not against their beliefs to welcome the media and use the opportunities it provides.

Aid organisations advertise their activities and encourage more people to get involved. This material is produced by Cafod/Christian Aid/Tear Fund.

INDEX